How to Fix Medicare

AEI STUDIES ON MEDICARE REFORM
Joseph Antos and Robert B. Helms
Series Editors

What ails Medicare is what ails health care in America. Medicare spending is growing substantially faster than we can afford, with potentially disastrous consequences for the federal budget. Worse, although the program is paying for more services, it is not necessarily providing better care for the elderly and the disabled. AEI's Studies on Medicare Reform is designed to examine the program's operation, consider alternative policy options, and develop a set of realistic proposals that could form the basis for reform legislation.

THE DIAGNOSIS AND TREATMENT OF MEDICARE
Andrew J. Rettenmaier and Thomas R. Saving

MARKETS WITHOUT MAGIC:
HOW COMPETITION MIGHT SAVE MEDICARE
Mark V. Pauly

HOW TO FIX MEDICARE:
LET'S PAY PATIENTS, NOT PHYSICIANS
Roger Feldman

How to Fix Medicare

Let's Pay Patients, Not Physicians

Roger Feldman

The AEI Press

Publisher for the American Enterprise Institute

WASHINGTON, D.C.

Distributed to the Trade by National Book Network, 15200 NBN Way, Blue Ridge Summit, PA 17214. To order call toll free 1-800-462-6420 or 1-717-794-3800. For all other inquiries please contact the AEI Press, 1150 Seventeenth Street, N.W., Washington, D.C. 20036 or call 1-800-862-5801.

Library of Congress Cataloging-in-Publication Data

Feldman, Roger D.
  How to fix Medicare : let's pay patients, not physicians / Roger Feldman.
    p. cm.
Includes bibliographical references.
    ISBN 13: 978-0-8447-4265-6 (pbk.)
    ISBN-10: 0-8447-4265-1
    1. Medicare. 2. Health care reform—Economic aspects—United States. 3. Insurance, Health—United States.
I. Title.
    [DNLM: 1. Medicare--economics. 2. Health Care Reform—economics—United States. WT 31 F312h 2008]

    RA412.3F45 2008
    368.38'200973—dc22

                                                    2008019986
12 11 10 09 08   1 2 3 4 5

Printed in the United States of America

Contents

List of Illustrations

Acknowledgments

In December 2004, the American Enterprise Institute for Public Policy Research (AEI) launched a program of research and publications to initiate a new debate about how to reform the Medicare program. Funding for this report, which is part of that debate, was provided by a subcontract from AEI to the author. The opinions expressed in the report are solely those of the author and do not represent the positions of AEI. The author would like to thank Ted Frech and Susan Feigenbaum for comments on an earlier draft and Joe Antos for carefully reading the report. All correspondence should be addressed to Roger Feldman at feldm002@umn.edu.

Introduction

Since its inception, Medicare has been deeply engaged in setting prices for hospitals and physicians. At first, this was done by mimicking the practices used by Blue Cross and some Blue Shield plans at the time Medicare was enacted, namely, paying hospitals' average costs and physicians' "customary, prevailing, and reasonable" charges.

During the 1980s (for hospitals) and 1990s (for physicians), Medicare discarded these initial approaches to setting prices and substituted prospective, diagnosis-related payments for hospitals and a fee schedule known as the "Resource-Based Relative Value Scale" (RBRVS) for paying physicians. The RBRVS attempts to base the fee for each service on the amount of work required to produce that service, objectively measured by the physician's time, mental effort and judgment, technical skill, physical effort, and stress. While most health-care economists would agree that the prices of physicians' services should be related to the work required to produce them, the RBRVS does not use market forces to determine the value of the physician's work. Instead, it controls the prices that physicians are paid for every billable service.[1] Similar price controls are applied to hospitals, which are prevented from billing patients more than Medicare's allowed payments. In 2006, Medicare controlled the prices of approximately two hundred billion dollars' worth of hospital and physician services, or 1.6 percent of the gross domestic product (GDP).[2]

A number of trenchant criticisms of Medicare's pricing policies (especially of the RBRVS) leave little doubt that the RBRVS units for physicians' services bear little relationship to the relative costs of producing the services in an efficient physician's practice (Hadley

1991; Baumgardner 1992). Aside from a very few proposals, however (Pauly 1971; Gianfrancesco 1983; Hadley 1984; Graboyes 2000), no one has suggested what seems obvious: Let's get rid of Medicare price-setting.

This monograph will argue that Medicare should stop paying physicians altogether and instead reimburse patients directly according to a predetermined set of indemnity payments. An indemnity is a fixed amount of money that is paid to an individual after the occurrence of a well-defined event. Automobile collision insurance is a type of indemnity payment that is familiar to almost everyone—it pays the policyholder a fixed amount of money that depends on the amount of damage from a collision to his or her automobile. Although less familiar, a Medicare indemnity would work the same way. It would pay the patient, not the doctor, a fixed amount of money depending on the patient's medical condition. My thesis is that Medicare indemnities would get the government out of the futile business of trying to determine how much to pay doctors and place patients in control of this decision. While I will illustrate this thesis with an analysis of physicians' prices for Medicare Part B services, the argument could be applied to hospitals (covered by Medicare Part A) as well.

Aside from slight effects resulting from an increase in income, individuals would use the same amount of medical care as they would when paying with their own money. Therefore, they would have an incentive to use the right amount of medical care and to shop for the best prices and types of care offered by alternative providers. Providers, in turn, would be able to set prices, which would vary according to their skill, the complexity of the service, and supply and demand conditions in the local market.

In contrast, traditional Medicare sets prices without regard to market conditions, resulting in prices that are too low for some doctors and services. In the extreme case, some services that patients would be willing to purchase are not covered at all. The program also prohibits doctors from charging Medicare patients more than a minimal amount above the fee schedule. The result is limited access to specialists and specialized or noncovered services and changes in the way care is provided that are often adverse (for example, a five-minute office visit for a frail elderly patient with multiple chronic diseases). Some Medicare prices are too high, inducing doctors to overuse services—and patients accept this out of ignorance and lack of any significant out-of-pocket cost (since nearly all have supplementary coverage that fills in copayments). Patients get both too little and too much care; it's a coincidence if the price happens to reflect the relative value of a service properly.

Indemnity insurance solves the mispricing problem that causes these adverse consequences. Assuming that the Medicare subsidy remains as generous as it is today, indemnities would allow beneficiaries to adjust their use of services until the cost of the marginal service is just worth the additional payment that a patient must make—that is what "the right amount of medical care" means. For many, that could mean no additional services (or better doctors) would be purchased, since the subsidy would cover adequate care. But other patients would gladly pay more out of pocket for better (in their view) treatment.

Obviously, patients need a better understanding of their treatment and provider alternatives than they now have. With indemnity coverage, however, they could hire a doctor as a real guide and adviser to the health system. Medicare prohibits such an arrangement today.

In the monograph that follows, chapter 1 presents the history of Medicare physician payment policy, from the inception of the program in 1965 through the implementation of a fee schedule in 1992 and subsequent attempts to control total Medicare Part B spending.

Chapter 2 analyzes the RBRVS fee schedule that Medicare currently uses to pay physicians. Although health economists generally agree that the goal of the fee schedule should be to simulate a perfectly functioning competitive market, there is also little doubt that the RBRVS does not succeed in meeting that goal; specifically, it is widely agreed that the RBRVS units for physicians' services bear little relationship to the relative minimum average costs of producing those services.

Chapter 3 describes several reforms that have been proposed, such as allowing unlimited "balance billing" by physicians or setting a single "global budget" for all Medicare-covered services in a defined geographic area. While some of these reforms may represent improvements over the current payment system, none will simulate the conditions of a competitive market. This will require a totally new direction for Medicare's physician payment policy.

Chapter 4 describes the new direction: indemnities, which are fixed amounts of money paid to the patient after the occurrence of a well-defined event. I describe the history of indemnities and of forerunners to my proposal for Medicare indemnities, including a successful federal demonstration of indemnities for long-term care services, and international experience with indemnities for episodes of acute illness. This is followed by my plan for designing a Medicare indemnity, along with acknowledgments of the problems that will arise and suggestions for solutions.

Chapter 5 argues that Medicare supplementary insurance must be banned in order for my proposal—or any proposal that uses prices to signal patients' preferences—to work. Chapter 6 discusses another hurdle that must be cleared before the market for physicians' services can reach the competitive equilibrium: the pervasive market power of physicians. I argue that strong enforcement of antitrust laws will be required to ensure providers do not have market power.

Finally, because indemnities represent a radical break from traditional methods of paying providers, in chapter 7 I recommend a demonstration of Medicare indemnities, and I describe some of the design features this demonstration should test.

The body of the monograph is followed by three appendices. Appendix 1 presents an economic model that explains why the RBRVS does not meet the goal of simulating a perfectly competitive market. This appendix can be skipped if the reader feels that the summary of the reasoning presented by chapter 2 is adequate. Appendix 2 discusses why it took more than twenty-five years to reform Medicare's original physician payment system, which was adopted hastily in 1965 and roundly criticized almost from its inception. Appendix 3 describes an innovative program, started in 1998, that allowed persons who were eligible for long-term care assistance to be responsible for directing their own care with indemnities.

This monograph does not discuss Medicare's overall financial condition, which some believe is in a state of crisis (Kotlikoff and Burns 2004). Medicare has many problems, not the least of which is its increasing costs and the lack of revenue to cover them. The proposals put forth here would not be less attractive, however, if Medicare were running a large intergenerational surplus rather than a deficit. This monograph is a blueprint for *smarter* Medicare payments, not *cheaper* payments. It is aimed at making Medicare better, a goal that is independent of the program's overall financial condition.

1

History of Medicare Physician Payment Policy

According to Philip Lee and Paul Ginsburg (1988), the legislation that created Medicare was passed in 1965 with limited time to settle on a method of paying physicians. In lieu of a detailed analysis of the question, Congress adopted payment policies designed to gain support from the medical profession, which had opposed including physicians' services in the Medicare program (Feldstein 2001, 249–53). The legislation specified that physicians would be paid according to the "usual, customary, and reasonable" (UCR) reimbursement system that had been used "largely on an experimental basis" by a few Blue Shield plans for a little more than a decade (Lee and Ginsburg 1988, 352).[1] Medicare changed the name of the payment system to "customary, prevailing, and reasonable" (CPR) reimbursement. This meant a physician's actual charge for a Medicare service would be subjected to two screens: The "customary" charge was what the physician had charged for the service during the previous year, while the "prevailing" charge was set at the seventy-fifth percentile of customary charges of other physicians in the same specialty and geographic area. The "reasonable" charge— what the physician would be paid—was the smallest of the actual charge, the customary charge, and the prevailing charge.[2] Beginning in 1972, annual increases in prevailing charges were limited to increases in the "Medicare Economic Index" (MEI), which measured physicians' practice costs.

During the 1980s, Congress began a series of actions designed to control rapid increases in Medicare Part B spending. In 1984 customary and prevailing fees for all physicians' services were frozen,

6

and when the freeze was lifted two years later, the prevailing fees for "participating" physicians were increased by 4 percent. (Participating physicians are those who agree to accept Medicare's reasonable fees as payment in full for all services they furnish to Medicare beneficiaries during the year.) In 1987 the freeze was lifted for all physicians, but nonparticipating physicians were subjected to limits on their maximum allowable charges for four more years.

Against this background, Congress created the Physician Payment Review Commission (PPRC) in 1986, with a broad mandate to advise Congress on "basic reform needed in physician payment" (Lee and Ginsburg 1988, 352). In its first *Report to Congress*, the PPRC (1987) recommended replacing the existing CPR payment system with a schedule of fees for each service. In its second report, issued March 31, 1988, the PPRC recommended basing the fees on the "relative value" of the work needed to produce each service. The particular definition of physician work was supplied by William Hsiao and colleagues at Harvard University (Hsiao et al. 1988). According to their conceptual framework, "work" consisted of the time, mental effort and judgment, technical skill, physical effort, and stress from iatrogenic risk (that is, the risk of a medical problem being caused by medical treatment) that went into producing each service. The relative value for each service was determined by multiplying total work for that service (TW) by an index (K) designed to adjust for relative practice costs and the amortized value of the opportunity cost of training across specialties:

(1) $RBRVS = TW \times K$

Allowed charges for Medicare physicians' services were defined as the lesser of the actual charge or the fee determined from the resource-based relative value scale (Hoffman, Klees, and Curtis 2000). Legislation to establish the Medicare fee schedule was enacted in the Omnibus Budget Reconciliation Act of 1989 (OBRA89), and, in January 1992, a four-year, phased implementation began.[3] The fee schedule took three years to develop and elicited more than 95,000 comments. When finally implemented, it covered approximately eight thousand distinct services (Levy et al. 1992).

In addition to setting relative fees, Medicare has attempted to control overall Part B spending through an "expenditure target" program that adjusts the fees up or down according to whether total expenditures fall below or exceed a target. Initially known as volume performance standards (VPS), the expenditure targets were replaced by the Balanced Budget Act of 1997 and the program renamed the "sustainable growth-rate" (SGR) system. Under SGR, the expenditure target is allowed to increase for inflation in physicians' practice costs, changes in enrollment in fee-for-service Medicare, changes in spending due to law and regulation, and growth in the real gross domestic product (Hackbarth 2005b). I will say more about the VPS/SGR system when I come to the topic of global budgets in chapter 3, which discusses proposed reforms of Medicare Part B.

Medicare Part B pays for many services in addition to those of physicians. Payments for durable medical equipment (DME) and clinical laboratory services are based on a fee schedule, and while hospital outpatient services and home health agencies historically were reimbursed on a "reasonable cost" basis, the Balanced Budget Act of 1997 provided for implementation of a prospective payment system for those services.

Part B payment for diagnostic imaging is different from other services and could best be described as both "in and out" of the fee schedule. If the test is performed in a facility such as a hospital outpatient department, the costs of equipment, supplies, and technician time are covered by a "facility payment." If the test is performed in a doctor's office, these costs are covered by a fee schedule known as the "technical component" (Medicare Payment Advisory Commission 2004b). Interpretation of the image by a physician is called the "professional component" and is reimbursed under the physician fee schedule regardless of where the test is performed. If the test is performed and interpreted by the same physician, the physician submits a global claim that includes both technical and professional components.

2

Goal and Flaws of Medicare Physician Payment Policy

Over the course of the decade preceding passage and implementation of the Medicare fee schedule, policy analysts came to a remarkable consensus over the goal of the program's physician payment policy. As the PPRC said in its second report, "A resource-cost basis can be seen as an attempt to simulate a perfectly functioning market. In such a market, competition drives relative prices to reflect the relative costs of efficient producers" (Physician Payment Review Commission 1988, 46). This sentiment was echoed by Joseph Antos, at that time director of the Office of Research and Demonstrations of the Health Care Financing Administration: "A fee schedule represents an administrative attempt to reproduce the information about supplies and demands for services that would be generated in a competitive market" (1991, 43).

Two independent analysts, Jack Hadley and James Baumgardner, explained why competition is the ideal goal for a physician payment system. As Hadley said, competition will lead to "equality between the price of a service and the minimum average cost of producing that service in an optimally scaled plant or firm" (1991, 102). Any third-party payer that wants to obtain services for its patients at the lowest cost will pursue this goal. And, according to Baumgardner, "The efficient competitive equilibrium prices that RBRVS seeks to mimic will clear the market for the respective procedures" (1992, 1028). In other words, patients will be indifferent at the margin between spending one more dollar on each service, and physicians will be indifferent at the margin between producing another unit of each service.

Why don't we rely on competition to get us to the efficient point in this market, as we do in many other markets in which the government does not set prices? The rationale behind the Medicare RBRVS is that the prices for physicians' services in the absence of controls are "distorted"—that is, if we form the ratio of two prices paid under Medicare, it will be different from the ratio found in a competitive market.[1] The price ratio is also known as the "relative price," so we can also say that the relative price of Medicare Part B services will be distorted in the absence of controls. According to the Physician Payment Review Commission (1989),

> Studies by the commission and others have shown that the current pattern of payments departs substantially from the actual resource costs of providing physician services. For example, physicians systematically receive less payment for evaluation and management services in relation to physician time and effort than they receive for invasive and imaging procedures (xiii).

Why should the prices of physicians' services under Medicare differ from the ideal competitive prices? There are problems on both the supply and the demand sides of the market for physicians' services. On the supply side, many analysts believe that physicians have market power—power to alter prices to their advantage—and that this power differs systematically across specialties, services, and geographic areas. Additional supply-side problems include constraints on the provision of medical care by non-physicians and restricted entry of new physicians. Given these problems, a large increase in demand for the services of a particular specialty may not cause the supply of that service to increase. Hence, the prices of services provided by that specialty will increase.

On the demand side, lack of information, insurance coverage, and "the special nature of medical care" (Hsiao and Dunn 1991, 222) mean that consumer demand is not fully informed, voluntary, or rational. If physicians are able to identify variations in patients' willingness to pay, they can "mark up" the prices of services for which demand is especially inelastic (for example, those with the deepest insurance coverage, or those about which consumers are least informed), often substantially higher than costs. The power to set high prices is especially pertinent for the prices of services provided by specialist physicians. Lee and Ginsburg described "a noticeable trend toward increasing expenditures for the services of specialists, particularly those who use considerable equipment when providing care" (1988, 353). Another study (Etheredge 1986) found that Medicare spending increases for general surgeons from 1975 to 1982 were largely the result of price increases at 15 percent per year rather than volume increases.

Among the most notable market failures in the Medicare program is the widespread presence of supplementary insurance that insulates patients from Medicare's cost-sharing requirements. Sandra Christensen and Judy Shinogle (1997) estimated that about 70 percent of beneficiaries have private insurance that supplements Medicare, while George Chulis, Franklin Eppig, and John Poisal (1995) estimated the supplementary coverage rate at 78 percent. In addition, 15 percent of Medicare beneficiaries receive full or limited Medicaid benefits, bringing the total market share of all Medicare beneficiaries with either private or public supplementary insurance to 85–93 percent.

Almost all researchers agree that supplementary insurance removes price from patients' calculations regarding the costs and benefits of using medical care, leading to consumption of more physicians' services than would be observed in its absence (Christensen, Long, and Rodgers 1987; Christensen and Shinogle 1997; Atherly 2002). This view is so widely held that it is almost an article of faith among health economists (Ginsburg 1983; McGuire 1991; Langwell 1993; Frech 1999).

Even Robert Ball, one of the architects of Medicare and its first administrator, shared the opinion that "Medicare is paying a heavy price as private insurance rests on top of the basic Medicare coverage" (1998, 37). The original framers of Medicare had no idea that this would happen. As Ball said, "We thought that the bills left uncovered were mostly too small to justify the administrative costs of supplementary insurance programs." But it did happen, and, to quote Ball again, "The result is that neither the patient nor the physician on behalf of the patient has an incentive to think twice about the cost of a procedure." I will pick up the topic of supplementary insurance again in chapter 5, with a simple proposal that such insurance be abolished.

Given that the market for Medicare physicians' services was failing in many ways, it is not surprising that the PPRC recommended, and Congress enacted, a new payment system that controls the price of every service supplied by physicians to Medicare. The seductive appeal of price controls arose because they appeared to be a way to correct the market failures in Medicare. Equally plausible was the idea that the Medicare fee schedule should be based on the resource costs of producing each service. As Jack Hadley and Robert Berenson aptly remarked, the health policy debate that preceded the introduction of the Medicare RBRVS resembled the debate among early Christian theologians over what constituted a "just price."[2] Almost everyone—patients, providers, and Congress—was unhappy with the way that Medicare paid physicians. There was considerable support for junking the old system and replacing it with one based on resource costs "in the belief that resource costs are more fixed, less manipulable, and less subject to distortion than market fees" (Hadley and Berenson 1987, 461). In other words, the RBRVS would provide the "just prices" that Baumgartner described. The market would clear, and no one would feel they could find a better set of services than the one they consumed or produced.

As Hadley pointed out, however, if the market were not competitive, there would be no reason to believe that the ratio of measured average costs for any pair of services would be a more accurate assessment of their relative value than the distorted ratio of their prices. The very factors that distort relative prices (differential demand in the presence of insurance, limited entry, and imperfect information) also distort relative average costs. Hadley explained the problem in these terms:

> One service may have an average cost close to the minimum of the average cost curve, for example, but a high

markup of price over average cost because of the nature of demand for that service. Another service, however, may be produced at an inefficient (high) level of average cost but have low markup of price over cost. Given non-constant markups, for any pair of services, the better approximation to the ideal relative value depends on the relative shapes of the average and marginal cost and revenue functions. A priori there is no reason to think that one is always closer to the ideal (1991, 111–12).

When we think about Medicare's physician price controls, the following question inevitably arises: Many private health plans pay physicians with fee schedules modeled on Medicare's RBRVS. If Medicare's prices are flawed, why isn't the same true when private payers use these prices to pay physicians? In a careful analysis of the differences between government price controls and private-sector payment systems, H. E. Frech III answered this question. According to Frech, "There are many safety valves for consumers and competitive constraints" on what private insurers can do in contracting for low prices (2000, 353). Most private plans include provisions for consumers who don't like the quality or accessibility of contracting physicians to purchase medical care from noncontracting physicians at a higher price. Many consumers can also switch to a different insurer, offering a different network of contracting providers and/or different terms. The ability of consumers to exploit these safety valves distinguishes private insurers who use fee schedules from the superficially similar RBRVS. This observation does not mean that I support the use of private-sector fee schedules to pay physicians. The private sector could also benefit from adopting the indemnity method of physician payment proposed in chapter 4. Nevertheless, whether or not private physician payment systems are properly designed, they are not price-control systems.

3

Not-So-Real Reforms

This chapter describes some reforms previously proposed for addressing the problems with Medicare's physician payment system (balance billing, physician diagnosis-related groups, capitation, and global budgets) and demonstrates why they won't work.

Balance Billing

Some critics of Medicare price controls (such as Frech in his 1996 study) have argued that the problems caused by an inaccurate RBRVS can be remedied by allowing unlimited balance billing—that is, letting physicians charge what they want in excess of the allowed fees and requiring patients to make up the difference. Advocates of balance billing argue that it would eliminate access problems because "any physician would be willing to treat any Medicare patient" (Frech 1996, 83). Also, widespread balance billing would signal that some procedures were underpriced, and if the system responded to those signals, the RBRVS could evolve into a more reasonable set of prices.

However, balance billing isn't all it's cracked up to be. To analyze the proposal, I will use a model that makes the following assumptions:

- One medical service is consumed by both Medicare and private patients, with the same marginal cost for either type of patient.

- Medicare patients have supplementary insurance that pays 100 percent of Medicare's reasonable charge for the service, but they are responsible for paying any bills in excess of the reasonable charge.

- Physicians who are allowed to balance-bill can charge different prices to different groups of Medicare patients and to private patients.[1]

- There are two types of physicians, distinguished by their overall capacity to see patients. This capacity can be measured by differences in the physicians' marginal cost functions. Those with "high" capacity have marginal cost MC, while those with "low" capacity have marginal cost MC*. If marginal costs are measured at the same quantity of services, MC* > MC.

At first glance, it might seem that all physicians will serve more Medicare patients when they can balance-bill. The ability to balance-bill, however, makes absolutely no difference in the total quantity of Medicare services supplied by high-capacity physicians. In the absence of balance billing, they will operate where private marginal revenue (MR) is equal to the Medicare fee and marginal cost (MC). As shown in figure 3-1, they will supply Q_P services to the private market and Q_M to the Medicare market. If unrestricted balance billing is allowed, these physicians will equalize on four margins: They will set MR equal to marginal revenue from balance billing Medicare and to the Medicare fee, and all of these will be equal to MC. The outer edge, or "envelope," of the physician's MR possibilities with balance billing is shown by the heavy line in figure 3-1. The total number of Medicare patients seen is still determined by the intersection of the Medicare fee and MC. Balance billing simply lets these physicians collect more revenue from less price-sensitive Medicare patients—for example, those with better supplementary insurance coverage.

Physicians with low capacity will increase their supply of Medicare services if they can balance-bill without restrictions. Prior to balance billing, they will supply Medicare services up to the point where MC* is equal to the Medicare fee. With balance billing, they would balance-bill all Medicare patients, but increase their supply of Medicare services. As shown in figure 3-2, they will expand Medicare supply until MR is equal to marginal revenue from balance billing Medicare, and both are equal to MC*.

FIGURE 3-1

BALANCE BILLING WITH NO CHANGE IN MEDICARE SERVICES

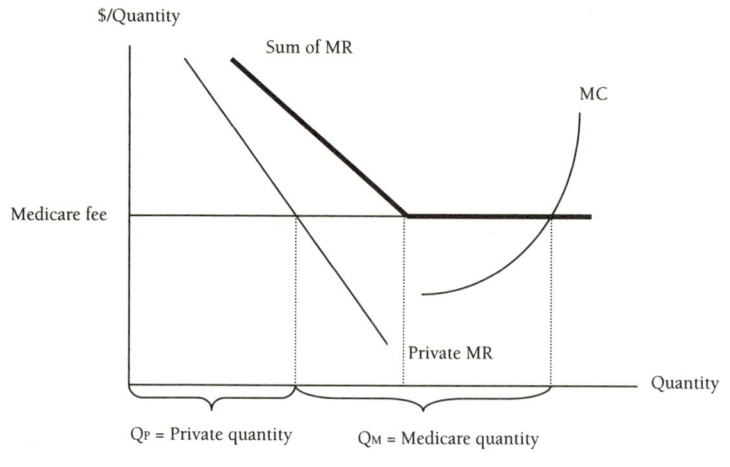

Source: Author's calculations.

Whether balance billing simply transfers revenue to physicians, as in figure 3-1, or increases the supply of Medicare services, as in figure 3-2, depends on the volume of services that physicians accept on assignment versus the volume for which they balance-bill. If most services are accepted on assignment (that is, the doctor accepts the Medicare fee as payment in full), then there would appear to be little efficiency gained from balance billing.

Data on Medicare assignment rates cast doubt on the need for balance billing on a large scale. In 2003, 99 percent of allowed Medicare charges were assigned. Moreover, physician participation and assignment rates in Medicare have been rising in recent years (Medicare Payment Advisory Commission 2004a).[2] These data, taken in conjunction with the rising rate at which physicians are accepting new Medicare patients and with MedPAC's surveys that show a narrowing gap between Medicare and private physician prices, suggest that the net marginal revenue from Medicare patients is not substantially different from that of privately insured patients.[3]

FIGURE 3-2
BALANCE BILLING WITH MORE MEDICARE SERVICES

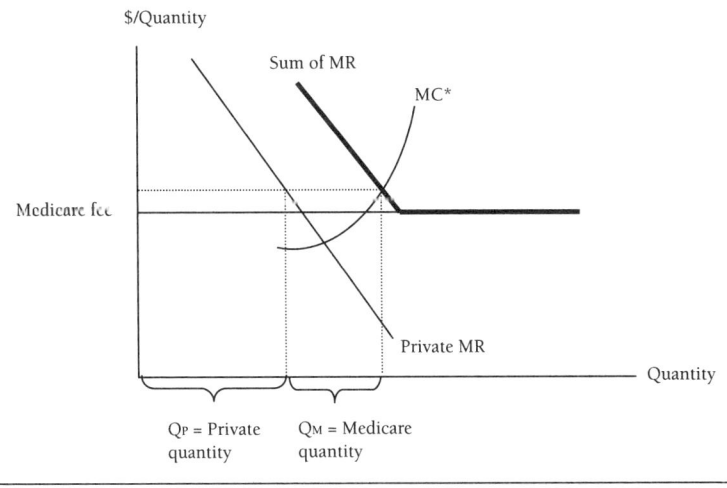

$/Quantity

Sum of MR

MC*

Medicare fee

Private MR

Quantity

Q_P = Private
quantity

Q_M = Medicare
quantity

Source: Author's calculations.

Physician Diagnosis-Related Groups

The idea behind paying physicians according to diagnosis-related groups (DRGs) is that payments for services of so-called "hospital-based physicians" (radiologists, pathologists, and anesthesiologists) are bundled together with payments for the hospital admissions in which the services are rendered. Physician DRGs were proposed by the Ronald Reagan administration in 1987. Needless to say, the affected physicians opposed the idea because it would have made them dependent on hospitals. As the American College of Radiologists said, "Radiologists would be much closer to being hospital employees than they now are" (Moorefield, MacEwan, and Sunshine 1993, 324). Mark Pauly and colleagues also doubted whether physicians would be eager to share their fees with suppliers of other inputs to the bundled services (1992, 150).

Such political opposition notwithstanding, physician DRGs have the same drawbacks as RBRVS fees: They are based on a standardized payment per case, "which can be thought of as the average cost of a Medicare case in an average, nonteaching, hospital" (Russell 1989, 11). There is no reason to think that average cost in an "average, nonteaching, hospital" comes closer to the minimum average cost of production in an efficient hospital than the average cost of physicians' services approaches the minimum average cost in an optimally scaled physician practice (Hadley 1991).

If, however, the hospital payment system did not attempt to mimic the average cost of a Medicare case, there would be a strong argument for "bundling" the payment for all aspects of the patient's care—including physicians, acute-care hospitals, and long-term care—into a single lump sum. Paying separately for physicians, hospitals, and nursing homes maintains the fiction that these treatment sites are separate and unrelated. In fact, patients and their providers may wish to substitute more resources toward one setting and less toward others. A bundled payment would make it easier to select the optimal treatment pattern.

Capitation

Under a capitation system, physicians are paid a predetermined amount for each patient for whom they are responsible. As applied to Medicare, physicians could be capitated separately from other providers of Medicare services (for example, with separate rates for hospitals and nursing homes), or a single capitated entity could be responsible for all services covered by Medicare.

My colleagues and I have analyzed Medicare capitation extensively in a book (Dowd, Feldman, and Christianson 1996) and numerous articles. Capitation was introduced into Medicare on a large scale by the Tax Equity and Fiscal Responsibility Act of 1982 (TEFRA). Final regulations to implement TEFRA were published in January 1985. Under TEFRA, prepaid health plans (mostly health maintenance organizations, or HMOs) were paid 95 percent of the cost of caring for an enrolled beneficiary had that beneficiary remained in fee-for-service (FFS) Medicare. Since FFS cost was not observed for beneficiaries choosing the HMO sector, it had to be estimated, and the estimate was obtained by calculating the cost of FFS enrollees who were similar to HMO enrollees with respect to age, gender, disability, Medicaid and institutional status, and county of residence.

We identified several problems with the Medicare capitation program as it was originally designed. One was that the administrative method used to determine the payment rates had little to do with HMOs' actual costs of providing the statutory Medicare benefits (Dowd, Coulam, and Feldman 2000).[4] In most cases, the payments were higher than HMOs' actual costs, leading them to provide many optional (that is, nonstatutory) benefits for little or no out-of-pocket premium. Because HMOs were not permitted to give the overpayments to enrollees in the form of premium rebates, some of the additional benefits were inefficient, in the sense that beneficiaries would not have been willing to pay as much as the benefits actually cost (Feldman et al. 2001; Pizer, Frakt, and Feldman 2003). A second problem was that the FFS system, with its open-ended expenditures, was protected from competition with the capitated plans.

The Medicare capitation program has been modified many times, and some of the problems we identified have been solved or at least mitigated. Since 2003, premium rebates to HMO enrollees have been permitted. Except for a "tax" that the HMO has to pay on the payment reduction, these premium rebates solve the problem of inefficient benefits in areas where the capitation payment is too high.

The capitation program was modified most recently by the Medicare Prescription Drug, Improvement, and Modernization Act of 2003 (MMA). As a short-term measure, the MMA added a new payment option of 100 percent of fee-for-service costs in 2004 and increased all payment rates by the growth in per-capita FFS Medicare spending in 2005. Since 2006, HMOs wanting to participate in Medicare have had to submit "bids" indicating the per-capita revenue at which they are willing to provide Part A and B services to Medicare. Medicare compares the bids against "benchmarks," which must be at least as great as per-capita FFS expenditures in each county and are higher than FFS expenditures in many counties. The benchmark for local plans (those choosing their own service areas) is a weighted average of the capitation rates for the service area. The benchmark for regional plans (those operating in service areas defined by Medicare), which otherwise operate under the same rules as local plans, is a blend of the weighted capitation rate for the region and a plan bid component that is a weighted average of all bids in the region.

Plans bidding less than the benchmarks are paid their bid, plus 75 percent of the difference between their bid and the benchmark. Plans must then return that 75 percent to beneficiaries in the form of extra benefits or Part B or Part D rebates.[5] Plans bidding above the benchmarks are paid the benchmark and must charge the difference between their bid and the benchmark to enrollees as an additional out-of-pocket premium.

The MMA bidding system for local plans—which are mainly HMOs—is flawed on two accounts. First, although the language of the MMA suggests a competitive bidding system, HMOs continue to be paid at rates that are set almost entirely administratively, just as they were before the MMA. The administratively set benchmarks in the HMO sector result in wide variation in the difference between the benchmark and average bids across counties. In counties where bids are lower than benchmarks and the difference is large, HMOs can afford to offer a rich package of premium rebates and extra benefits—even some with limited appeal to beneficiaries. In other counties such benefits are not available. If HMO payments were linked more tightly to average bids, the allocation of Medicare benefits across plan types and counties would be both more equitable and more cost-effective. In contrast, regional plans—including prescription drug plans (PDPs)—are paid relative to a benchmark that is a function of the average bid. In principle, at least, this crucial distinction should make price competition among PDPs much more intense than among HMOs.

The second flaw of the local bidding system, which is shared by regional bidding, is that neither system solves the last problem identified by Dowd, Feldman, and Christianson (1996): Fee-for-service Medicare is exempt from the competitive bidding system, at least until 2010. In that year, a six-year demonstration of competitive bidding known as the Comparative Cost Adjustment (CCA) program is scheduled to begin in at least six metropolitan statistical areas (MSAs). Demonstration sites will be chosen from among MSAs that have two or more local private plans with at least 25 percent total penetration. A benchmark local premium will be set by the enrollment-weighted average of the bids by private plans and FFS Medicare. If a plan—including FFS Medicare—bids above the benchmark, the beneficiary will pay the difference between the plan's bid and the benchmark. Although FFS beneficiaries will be partially protected from competition by a restriction that their premium cannot change by more than 5 percent in any given year, this program, if allowed to proceed as scheduled, will bring FFS Medicare into the competitive fray for the first time.[6]

Capitation has the potential to be a powerful method for determining how much to pay Medicare health plans, including traditional fee-for-service Medicare. In our book, we recommended that Medicare take bids and set the government contribution to premiums equal to the lowest bid submitted by a qualified plan in a local market area (Dowd, Feldman, and Christianson 1996, 67). Beneficiaries would be responsible for paying the difference between the low bid and the premiums charged by higher bidders.

Under a capitated payment system, Medicare does not worry about how much to pay providers. That is left up to the health plans, which are free to experiment with different payment systems, including fee-for-service, salary, and risk-sharing arrangements with physicians. Although it promotes such experimentation, however, capitation cannot be a complete solution to Medicare's problem of paying providers. In the first place, capitated health plans do not serve all areas of the country. In sparsely populated rural areas, in particular, low population density and high entry costs make it difficult to form networks of health-care providers. (This is also a limitation of the global budget system, discussed next.) In addition, in areas where capitated plans compete with traditional Medicare, many beneficiaries will choose the traditional program. Finally, the politics of capitation are extremely contentious, and it is questionable whether the Comparative Cost Adjustment demonstration will be implemented at all, let alone as a national payment system.[7]

Global Budgets

From time to time, proposals have surfaced calling for "areawide payment incentives" for physicians. Under these proposals, geographic market areas would be designated, and within them targets would be set for total Medicare Part A and Part B expenditures. Physicians in a given area would be rewarded or penalized depending on how close aggregate charges came to these targets. I refer to these proposals as "global budgets" for all Medicare services in given geographic areas.

The rationales behind these proposals have varied. In an early proposal, Peter Fox (1984) argued that global budgets are the only way to address the "blank-check mentality" associated with fee-for-service Medicare. More recently, John Wennberg and colleagues have observed that Medicare spending per capita in some regions of the United States is more than twice as high as in other regions, with no obvious improvements in compliance with the standards of medical practice recommended by evidence-based medicine. Wennberg et al. (2002) maintain that regional budget caps benchmarked to the low-cost areas could save Medicare $40 billion per year after adjusting for regional spending differences related to age, sex, and illness.

These global budget proposals appear to be a logical extension of capitation to a more expansive geographic area. This analogy is valid in part, which implies that global budgets share the same drawbacks as capitation payments to private plans in Medicare. Among them is the administrative formula used to determine the payment level. Fox (1984) advocated adjusting the target level only for the age composition of beneficiaries within the area, with annual increases initially tied to historical rates of increase in Medicare expenditures. Basing the rates of increase on historical trends obviously would build Medicare's past inefficiencies into future payment rates, but Fox thought the increases would moderate over time if the areawide incentives were successful. In Wennberg's proposal, the capitation payments would be based on the same factors (with the addition of the regional illness burden) that were used until recently to pay local HMOs.

In addition to the problems with local capitation, the global budget proposal is missing a piece. As Hadley said, "A basic flaw in the design of the areawide incentive approach is that it lacks a mechanism for forcing individual physicians to follow the group incentive" (1984, 122). In the absence of compulsion, individual physicians always will do better by pursuing their own financial interests. This will contribute to the deficit; but since each physician bears only a small part of that cost, he or she will disregard the areawide expenditure target.

This concern was repeated recently by Glenn Hackbarth, chairman of MedPAC, in describing Medicare's efforts to control Part B spending through the sustainable growth-rate system:

> The underlying assumption of an expenditure control approach, such as the SGR, is that increasing updates [that is, periodic adjustments to the fee schedule that bring actual expenditures in line with budgeted expenditures] if overall volume is controlled, and decreasing updates if overall volume is not controlled, provides physicians nationally a collective incentive to control the volume of services. However, this assumption is incorrect because physicians do not respond to collective incentives but individual incentives. An efficient physician who reduces volume does not realize a proportionate increase in revenues. In fact, an individual physician has an incentive to increase volume (Hackbarth 2005a, 3).

If physicians learn over time that their efforts to "game the system" are self-defeating, they might learn not to disregard the expenditure target. According to Pauly and others, "In a world of foresighted physicians, the price (and volume) will immediately collapse to as low a price as is needed to reach the target level of expenditure" (1992, 133). However, if physicians' services are substitutes or complements for other services (including hospital services), adverse effects on total spending may result. For example, if price reductions for physician services cause physicians to substitute more drug prescriptions for those services, total costs could be adversely affected. In addition, it is doubtful that physicians could internalize the incentives to keep their expenditures within the target.

Wennberg and colleagues were aware that a global payment system would generate "perverse incentive effects" (2002, W105). They proposed, therefore, that Comprehensive Centers for Medical Excellence (CCMEs), based on hospitals, provider networks, or organizations representing regional coalitions, be established in each region to manage the capitation payments. To qualify, a CCME would have to establish best-practice models of medical care. Staff- and group-model HMOS that employ salaried physicians would be the best models for these organizations.

For CCMEs to constitute a national program, however, they would have to be established in every region of the country. This would be problematic because staff- and group-model HMOs have not been able to thrive except in areas with high population and physician densities. It would be extremely difficult to form these HMOs in rural areas.

Another problem is that successful CCMEs easily could become local monopolists. In Feldman and Lobo (1997), we showed that monopolists paid by global budgets may supply too few services, resulting in long waiting lines.[8] Waiting lines have developed in such global budget organizations as the U.S. Veterans Administration medical service and foreign national health services (Feldman 1994). I do not see how they could be prevented in a regional capitation system.

In practice, neither SGR nor its predecessor, VPS (volume performance standards), has performed as hoped. From 1980 through 1989, according to Hackbarth (2005b), annual growth in Part B spending per beneficiary, adjusted for inflation, ranged from a low of 1.3 percent to a high of 15.2 percent, with a mean of 8.0 percent. This is not a record to which to aspire. The SGR formula also produced volatile updates, Hackbarth wrote, which in 2003 led Congress to replace the GDP factor with a ten-year rolling average of GDP growth. Furthermore, volume continued to grow strongly even in years when the updates were small or negative. Finally, growth in volume per beneficiary varied widely across services, with the highest growth of 45 percent from 1999 to 2003 found in diagnostic imaging services (Hackbarth 2005b, 3, 5).

Poor performance aside, a global budget program would face exceptional political obstacles. Unless all doctors were included in the CCME—which would defeat the purpose of promoting CCMEs as "centers of excellence" for high-quality care—the excluded physicians would be barred from participating in Medicare. This would violate section 1802, title XVIII, of the Social Security Act (U.S. Social Security Administration 2008), which states that any willing provider must be accepted by Medicare:

> (a) BASIC FREEDOM OF CHOICE—Any individual entitled to insurance benefits under this title may obtain health services from any institution, agency, or person qualified to participate under this title if such institution, agency, or person undertakes to provide him such services (42 U.S.C. 1395a).

To implement the CCME program, section 1802 would have to be amended to exclude providers not affiliated with CCMEs. This would cause a firestorm of protest from the medical profession and from excluded hospitals whose survival would be threatened by withdrawal of Medicare patients. One possible alternative would be to designate the CCME as a "preferred provider" for Medicare (that is, Medicare patients could use the CCME under preferred terms). Medicare's efforts to encourage entry of regional preferred provider organizations (PPOs) have, however, not been successful to date (Pizer, Feldman, and Frakt 2005). Further subsidies appear to be needed to entice regional PPOs into Medicare, which could defeat any cost-saving potential from the CCME program.

4

Real Reform—Medicare Indemnities

Now that we have examined a number of proposals for reforms and their shortcomings, it is time to propose something different: real reform with Medicare indemnities. This chapter will introduce the concept of an indemnity and explain why medical indemnities would correct the perverse incentives created by the prevailing payment methods in health insurance. After describing how indemnities have been used for long-term care and the Republic of Korea to pay for medical care, I will offer a plan for designing a medical indemnity for Medicare.

Introduction to Indemnities

An indemnity is a fixed amount of money paid to an individual after the occurrence of a well-defined event. Indemnities are common in automobile and homeowners' insurance, which pay on the basis of damages to the policyholder's automobile or house. In the case of automobile insurance, the policyholder typically receives an appraisal of the damage from the insurance company in an amount sufficient to complete the repair if a company-approved repair shop is used. Sometimes the appraisal can be obtained by the policyholder him- or herself by submitting several estimates from approved repair shops to the company. After they agree on the appraisal, the company writes a check to the policyholder, and then withdraws entirely from oversight of the actual repair. The policyholder is free to obtain the repair from one of the approved repair shops, from someone else, or to make no repair at all. Through these choices, the policyholder reveals how much the repair is worth to him.

In the case of medical insurance, indemnity payments would be made after a particular illness was diagnosed. Patients would then be free to use the money to select the optimal course of treatment. The payment could be limited to the care obtained from physicians, or, as described in chapter 3 above, services obtained from multiple providers could be bundled into a single payment.

The merits of indemnity insurance for health care were discovered by a small number of policy analysts, including Mark Pauly, Frank Gianfrancesco, and Jack Hadley. Their early explorations were followed by Susan Feigenbaum's proposal to model health insurance on auto collision insurance. To my knowledge, Feigenbaum's 1992 proposal is the most recent for medical indemnities.

Mark Pauly (1971) described the perverse incentives created by the prevailing payment methods in health insurance: "An individual receives medical benefits only when he takes medical care, and the more he gets, and the more costly and expensive the care is, the larger the benefits he gets" (54–55). In contrast, a "pure" indemnity would specify the payment of a particular number of dollars to an individual with a given physical condition. Except for minor effects resulting from an increase in his income, the individual would consume the same amount of medical care as he would when paying with his own money. As a consequence, he would have an incentive to use the right amount of medical care and to shop for the best prices and types of care offered by alternative providers. Providers in turn would have incentives to become more efficient in order to gain business from indemnified consumers.

Frank Gianfrancesco (1983) was the second economist to analyze indemnity insurance for medical care. He added several more advantages of indemnities to Pauly's argument that they would create incentives for patients to use the right amount of medical care. First, he said, indemnities would make it easier for the *insurer* to predict its expenses because the variation in outlays "is unaffected by the variability of individual expenditures within each claim category" (177). This would lead to lower administrative costs. Second, indemnities would lead to a more equitable *distribution* of insurance benefits among similarly insured individuals because each would be paid the same amount. In contrast, most conventional insurance makes larger payments to physicians who treat patients more intensively. This is a variation of Pauly's criticism of traditional medical insurance.

Jack Hadley was the third economist to analyze indemnity insurance for medical care. His definition of an indemnity was different from Pauly's. Hadley viewed the indemnity as a fixed payment for each service, not a fixed payment triggered by the onset of a medical condition. He saw three advantages of per-service indemnities over a Medicare fee schedule. First, indemnities would reward patients for seeking care from lower-priced physicians; second, indemnities would not eliminate price competition among physicians; and third, indemnities would leave physicians free to change their fees when practice costs changed. The third point was particularly important because the difference between indemnity payments and physicians' actual charges could be a "barometer of how much access and quality beneficiaries are receiving" (Hadley 1984, 126).

Hadley also thought that an indemnity payment system would be easier to administer than the "customary, prevailing, and reasonable" reimbursement method, in which insurers had to perform complicated administrative calculations for every physician and claim. Physicians would set their own prices (and possibly be required to post them for customers to inspect), and billing arrangements would be left up to the physician. "If the bill were less than the indemnity, then the patient would receive the difference, less any cost-sharing," Hadley wrote (1984, 127).

In 1992, Susan Feigenbaum argued that the "central problem" facing our medical care system is that "consumers currently bear little of the cost of their utilization decisions" (1). Like Pauly, she attributed this problem to a medical insurance system that reduces the consumer's out-of-pocket price and increases the demand for medical care. To remedy it, she proposed replacing medical reimbursement insurance with a system of pure indemnities similar to auto collision insurance. In her ideal system, the subscriber's insurance company would conduct "claims appraisals" similar to those performed by an auto insurer. Upon determining that the patient's diagnosis was valid, the insurer would issue a lump-sum payment that would be accepted by contracting providers as payment in full for treatment. The critical distinction between the present insurance system and her proposed model is that "by paying insureds directly, diagnosis is divorced from the ensuing medical care, thereby reducing moral hazard on the part of providers and allowing subscribers to benefit from acting as prudent purchasers" (Feigenbaum 1992, 3).

Feigenbaum was aware that recipients of auto collision indemnities do not have to purchase any repair services, and she asked if there were any situations where patients might be able to spend their medical indemnities on nonmedical goods and services. One such case might be end-of-life medical care, where "one suspects that the same dollars put in the hands of the ill might be spent in a substantially different way" (4). Feigenbaum suggested that the individual would have to obtain "informed consent" before opting out of medical care. This would reduce the chance that he or she could later appeal to public or private subsidy programs to cover the cost of treatment. After introducing my proposal for indemnities, I will turn Feigenbaum's question around and ask if there are any conditions under which insured individuals might be *compelled* to buy medical care. I will also discuss the problem of enforcing indemnity contracts.

Following Feigenbaum, several studies investigated the properties of an "ideal" insurance policy—that is, one that would equate the marginal utility of a dollar paid at the point of purchasing medical care to that of a dollar paid at the point of purchasing insurance. David Cummins and Olivier Mahul (2004) asked if the ideal policy would have a deductible if there were an upper limit on coverage. Kenneth Arrow (1971) had shown that if the insurer charges a "loading fee" (a cost to process each claim), the optimal policy would have a deductible to discourage small claims, followed by full insurance above the deductible. Cummins and Mahul also showed that an ideal insurance policy with a limit on coverage would include a deductible and then full coverage up to the cap. But, unlike in Arrow's analysis, the policy would have a deductible even in the absence of administrative expenses. The intuition behind this result is that "raising the deductible reduces the premium and thus increases the amount of wealth available in states of the world when the policy limit constraint is binding" (Cummins and Mahul 2004, 254).

Finally, in a very extensive analysis that summarized the earlier literature, Robert Graboyes (2000) reviewed the potential for indemnity insurance. Assuming only one disease and an exogenous cure rate that varies in the population, he showed that it is never socially or privately optimal to offer an indemnity larger than the cost of treatment.

Why Aren't Indemnities Used in Medical Insurance?

If indemnity insurance is such a great idea, why hasn't it displaced traditional medical insurance? Pauly offered two explanations. First, because indemnity insurance creates incentives for providers to be efficient, and because providers also see patients with traditional insurance, some of the benefits of indemnity insurance will be captured by patients with traditional insurance. Any costs associated with the use of indemnity insurance "may exceed efficiency benefits for the individual, even though the benefits to all individuals exceed costs" (Pauly 1971, 56). Second, Pauly explained, there is a significant private cost of using indemnity insurance—the inability to specify precisely the severity of the condition for which a payment is made.[1] This leaves individuals exposed to the risk that they will not receive adequate compensation after developing a severe case of the condition. In contrast, traditional "cost coverage" insurance does provide protection against severity risk. Pauly proposed an alternative approach to a "pure" indemnity, combining a set payment with partial coverage of the risk that charges will exceed the indemnity level. I want to withhold further description of these "partial indemnity" systems until I get to the discussion of how indemnities might be designed for Medicare.

Interestingly, Gianfrancesco made light of the problems with indemnity insurance noted by Pauly, stating that "the information necessary to classify patient claims is, for the most part, contained in patient medical records" (1983, 182). He also thought it would be easy to detect fraudulent submission of claims through misspecification of the information contained in the medical record. While it is too early to discuss the issue of claims verification in detail, the evidence from other insurance markets—especially automobile insurance—suggests that verification can be difficult. A cursory examination of the literature indicates that automobile insurance is rife with moral hazard. For example, holders of car insurance policies with a "total replacement" provision (the opportunity to get a new vehicle in the event of theft or total destruction of the car within a specified period) have a higher probability of theft near the end of this protection period (Dionne and Gagne 2002).

Despite Gianfrancesco's assertions that it is relatively easy to design an indemnity policy, indemnities are not used in medical insurance, aside from personal accident policies that provide coverage for a few well-defined events (for example, a broken arm or loss of an eye). Instead, almost all medical insurance "pays off" by subsidizing the price of treatments obtained from licensed providers. Is this because indemnities are impractical or somehow inferior to standard medical insurance policies, or can we attribute their absence to other reasons?

To answer this question, I relied on Feigenbaum's history of indemnities for covering lost income and medical expenses.[2] As reviewed by Feigenbaum, the evidence indicates that indemnities once existed, but they were driven out of the market by the concerted opposition of hospitals and physicians who favored "traditional" insurance for financial reasons. Changing medical technology might have played a role in the disappearance of medical indemnities, but it was not the primary explanation.

Feigenbaum wrote, "In the first decade of [the twentieth] century voluntary mutual societies underwrote large numbers of 'sickness' policies, offering workers a means by which they could indemnify themselves for income losses due to adverse health events" (1). Although some insurers provided similar coverage for medical costs, only 1 percent of the $97 million in "sickness" benefits paid in 1914 went for medical care. The income loss from illness and accidents was much larger and more threatening to a worker's livelihood than the paltry cost of medical care, which was largely ineffective, in any case.

Feigenbaum offered two possible explanations for the decline of sickness insurance. The first was the rise in cost and complexity of medical care, which surpassed income replacement as an important insurable event. Feigenbaum was skeptical of this explanation. She observed that even in 1930, only 10 percent of benefits under then existing "health insurance" plans were spent on medical care, while 90 percent went toward replacing lost income.

Feigenbaum's second explanation relied on a political-economic argument: Sickness insurance declined because providers had a vested interest in developing their own insurance plans that linked benefits to subsidized medical care. The story of provider-sponsored health insurance has been told elsewhere (Goldberg and Greenberg 1977; Frech 1996), so I don't need to repeat it in detail here. Quite simply, medical providers (first hospitals and later physicians) sponsored their own insurance plans, which divided up the geographic territory into noncompeting areas, with one Blue Cross and one Blue Shield plan in each area. The admitted goal of the "Blues" was to stimulate demand for hospital services and to reduce payment defaults (Feigenbaum 1992). At the same time, the provider-sponsored plans pursued political protection from state legislatures in the form of favorable regulations and exemption from state premium taxes. To compete with the "Blues," commercial insurers reluctantly adopted similar payment practices. Favorable tax policies—first an exemption of health insurance from wartime wage controls and later favorable income-tax treatment of employer-paid premiums—cemented the link between health insurance and costly subsidies for medical care. Indemnity insurance survives today only in personal accident policies, some dental insurance plans, and "dread disease" policies that offer lump-sum payments in the event of diagnosis of certain diseases, such as cancer.

George and J. C. Herbert Emery offered a third explanation for the decline of sickness insurance, focusing on the role of the voluntary societies that offered this type of policy in the early part of the twentieth century. In their book, *A Young Man's Benefit* (1999), the Emerys documented the role of friendly societies in providing "sickness" insurance against income loss. These organizations once were a major source of such insurance in Canada and the United States. Medical costs associated with illness were much less important than lost income, as Feigenbaum had explained; and because neither commercial insurance companies nor the government provided disability insurance, voluntary fraternal organizations such as the Independent Order of Odd Fellows (IOOF) provided income replacement when an individual was sick and unable to work.

The Emerys attributed the decline in the importance of fraternal insurers to diminished demand by their members for income-replacement insurance as Canadian and U.S. households accumulated wealth and developed the capacity to self-insure. The Great Depression and subsequent poor labor market conditions in both countries in the 1930s hampered this ability, which led in the United States to the passage of government income-replacement programs, such as Social Security Disability Insurance and workers' compensation.

Long-Term Care Indemnities

One way in which indemnities have been tried with some success— at least in demonstrations—is to pay for long-term care benefits. Long-term care provides a favorable setting for using indemnities because the services each eligible person wants to use may be quite different, and designing a service-based reimbursement approach to meet these diverse preferences could be excessively complex. Furthermore, such indemnities do not become obsolete as the nature and scope of services change over time. As Robyn Stone (2001) wrote in an informative discussion of long-term care indemnities, "This model provides resources directly to individuals through a cash benefit or some type of a voucher system. Receipt of the benefits is triggered by some level of disability or other need for long-term care."[3] Illustrating the flexibility offered by long-term care indemnities, Stone continued: "The disability approach also provides resources that family caregivers can use to purchase complementary services or supports. They may decide, for example, to pay for evening and weekend respite care, services that are generally not available through care packages defined by public programs or private insurers" (99–100).

Stone reviewed several federal and state programs that use indemnities for long-term care benefits. At the federal level, the U.S. Department of Veterans Affairs' Housebound Aid and Attendance Allowance Program provides cash grants to veterans and their surviving spouses who are disabled and need long-term care in the community. According to Stone, "In 2001 a single veteran qualifying for this benefit was entitled to a monthly payment of $518 in addition to the regular pension of $775" (Stone 2001, 101).

At the state level, researchers at the National Council on Aging identified numerous long-term care indemnity programs. According to Stone, the most ambitious of these was the Cash and Counseling Demonstration and Evaluation, initiated to test the efficiency of "cashing out" Medicaid-funded home and community-based care services. Participating states obtained waivers to allow the payment of cash allowances in lieu of a service package. Preliminary results of the evaluation indicated that "more than 90 percent of the participants hired family members, friends, or neighbors to provide personal care services. . . . More than nine out of ten participants (including disenrollees from the cash group) indicated that they would recommend the cash option to others seeking greater control over their personal care decisions" (Stone 2001, 102). More detail on this unusual and innovative program is provided in appendix 3.

Stone also mentioned that a number of European countries, including Austria, France, Germany, and the Netherlands, use the indemnity approach to provide part or all of their long-term care benefits. The largest program, in Germany, lets beneficiaries living in the community select a cash indemnity, agency services set at twice the value of the indemnity, or a combination of the two. Despite the high "tax" on the indemnity compared with service benefits, 76 percent of the eligible population chose the indemnity in 1998.

In a sympathetic review of Stone's paper, Mark Pauly (2001) reinforced the idea that indemnity payments, in theory, are the best kind of insurance to have because they provide maximum flexibility on how to use the benefit, and they give the policyholder ideal incentives to consider the costs as well as the benefits of treatment.[4] He noted, however, a significant drawback of long-term care indemnities (which Stone also recognized): the problem of verifying eligibility. Pauly wrote that "insurers are terrified by the thought that if people can make money from insurance and do not have to do anything that healthy people would not do, there will be very substantial (and very clever) excess claims" (2001, 110). This problem is especially severe for long-term care, where many of the services (for instance, assistance with cleaning and cooking) would be desired by healthy people as well as those who are sick. Pauly noted that the private sector has been very reluctant to sell long-term care indemnity policies.

These observations point to a problem (possibly a dilemma) with indemnities. The conditions under which indemnities make the most sense are those in which individuals have a high degree of personal discretion over the choice of a treatment plan. But some of the services in these highly personal plans are likely to be "low-tech" items, such as home care or alternative medicine. As Pauly noted, these are also the types of services that are likely to be valued by healthy people; thus, the verification problem arises. The types of conditions for which indemnities are most practical (for example, a broken arm) are easy to verify, but patients have less discretion over their treatment plans and, therefore, may not value the freedom of choice offered by the indemnity. Further discussion of this problem and possible solutions may be found in chapter 7, which proposes a demonstration of indemnities for Medicare.

Indemnity Health Insurance in Korea

Despite its lack of acceptance in the United States, indemnity insurance is the most prevalent form of private health insurance in the Republic of Korea. About 30–40 percent of the population was enrolled in medical indemnity policies in 2002–3, increasing to 80 percent in 2006 (Kang, Kwon, and Yoo 2005). These policies pay a lump-sum amount of money in the case of a well-defined illness, typically for the first diagnosis of cancer. In 2005, 8 billion U.S. dollars, or 1.1 percent of the Korean gross domestic product, flowed through indemnity insurance. This compares with about 24 billion U.S. dollars in the Korean national health insurance (NHI) system.

One purveyor of indemnity insurance in Korea is American International Group Inc. (AIG), which sells policies that pay a lump-sum benefit if the insured is diagnosed for the first time with cancer during the policy year. In addition to this core coverage, the policies may provide daily hospital cash benefits and surgical expense reimbursement. The policies can be purchased by individuals or made available to employees as a fringe benefit. They can be offered alone or in combination with other benefits.

The Korean health system has several unique features not found in the United States that favor indemnity insurance. One of these is its unified fee system. Direct negotiations (that is, contracts to set fees) between hospitals and private insurers are not allowed. This means that one of the drawbacks of indemnities—private insurers' inability to negotiate prices with providers—is absent from the Korean system. Another feature is Korea's national health insurance system, which started in 1989 with poor benefits. While benefits offered by the NHI have improved, they still are not comprehensive. Patients are exposed to large out-of-pocket costs and financial risks. Thus, the indemnity insurance system in Korea is really a form of supplementary insurance that sits on top of the NHI. It does not totally replace it, as the indemnities proposed in this study would do for Medicare physician fees.

Despite these differences, Korean-style indemnity insurance may gain a foothold in the United States. Since 2006, the Conseco Insurance Company has sold a supplementary policy that pays a lump-sum benefit on the first diagnosis of cancer (Conseco 2008). The policy offers two plan options which pay benefit amounts ranging from $10,000 to $50,000.

My Proposal

Now that we have reviewed the principles and some of the history and applications of indemnity insurance, I will offer my proposal for Medicare indemnities. I will ascertain how much risk would be involved with indemnities, and how this risk could be reduced to a manageable level. After discussing how the occurrence of a costly event would be verified, I will explore the question of whether the indemnity should be restricted to medical care.

The Primary Argument for Indemnity Insurance. I propose that Medicare scrap the RBRVS physician payment system and replace it with "Medicare indemnities" that would pay patients a fixed amount of money depending on the diagnosis of a particular medical condition. Patients would be able to use the indemnity to purchase medical care from any provider under any terms and conditions the patients and providers find mutually satisfactory. Under some conditions, discussed below, they might be allowed to cash in part of the indemnity, as well.

The primary reason I believe indemnities would be superior to the current Medicare fee schedule is that they would reward patients who seek less costly care. With an indemnity policy, the cost of medical care is paid out-of-pocket, compared with the coinsurance policy, where the patient pays only a fraction of the cost out-of-pocket. Thus, the last dollar of medical care spent under the indemnity policy is worth one dollar to consumers, whereas the last dollar of medical spending under the coinsurance policy is worth only a fraction of a dollar. This is the same case made by Pauly in 1971: Having received an indemnity payment, an individual would consume the same amount of medical care as he would when paying with his own money. As a consequence, he would have an incentive to use the right amount of medical care and to shop for the best prices and types of care offered by alternative providers.

Consider the situation shown in figure 4-1, which compares a "budget-neutral" indemnity policy with a traditional insurance policy that uses coinsurance. Both policies start from the same consumer budget, shown by the heavy black line. For a small premium relative to the medical expense, the traditional policy reduces the consumer's out-of-pocket price of medical care (along the less steeply sloped dashed line), leading to an increase in consumption of medical care. In contrast, the indemnity policy for the same premium

FIGURE 4-1
INDEMNITY INSURANCE COMPARED WITH COINSURANCE

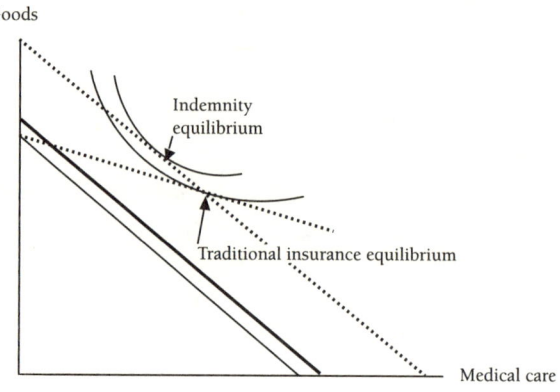

Source: Author's calculations.

transfers income to the consumer but does not change the relative price of medical care, as shown by the second dashed line, which is parallel to the budget line.[5] As a result, the consumer uses less medical care than with the traditional policy and reaches a higher level of utility. This is shown by the fact that the indemnity equilibrium point touches a higher indifference curve than does the equilibrium point for the traditional policy.

How to Design a Medicare Indemnity. Many issues would need to be addressed in order to design a practical Medicare indemnity. The first of these is the question of how to set the indemnity in relation to the expected costs of treatment. Gianfrancesco (1983) recommended a process of "trial and error," where the insurer attempts to set the indemnity equal to the modal expenditure associated with that category of service under traditional insurance. Patients who seek care from providers who charge less than the modal payment could keep the difference.

When we add other payers to the market, however—for example, patients under age sixty-five with private insurance—the situation becomes more complicated. In some cases, the indemnity payment might be more than enough to pay the physician's total bill, while in others it would be less than the modal expenditure, and patients would be balance-billed for the difference. Which case is relevant depends on the same conditions that determine the extent of balance billing under the current Medicare fee schedule. When physicians have "low capacity," and demand from other payers is added to the model, the market price for the modal treatment may exceed the indemnity payment, and Medicare patients would be balance-billed. In contrast, when physicians' capacity is high, patients would be able to cash in the unused portion of the indemnity.

Because providers' marginal costs and market demand conditions vary among geographic markets, the indemnity payments should be adjusted for these variations (Dowd et al. 2006–7). Medicare currently relies on three Geographic Practice Cost Indexes (GPCIs) to adjust the fee-schedule prices for local variation in the cost of physicians' work, practice expense, and professional liability insurance (Medicare Payment Advisory Commission 2003a).[6] However, there are only eighty-nine GPCI local market areas for the entire United States. This is well below the number of local markets that would be defined by patients' willingness to travel to obtain physicians' services. If Medicare moved to an indemnity payment system, it would be necessary to explore new market definitions that correspond more closely to geographic markets for physician services. Dowd et al. (2006–7) also discussed demand factors, such as illness burden and per-capita income, that influence Medicare spending in local markets. Efficient pricing requires that adjustments be made for these factors, as well as for differences in physicians' practice costs across markets.

A problem closely related to geographic adjustment is how to adjust the indemnity for changes in medical technology. It should be noted that all third-party payers, including competitive private insurers, face the same problem.[7] One possible response is for Medicare to observe the adjustments that private payers make to their physician fees.

With all of these adjustments, wouldn't Medicare indemnities wind up looking like the RBRVS system with its thousands of codes, which for all practical purposes has been captured by the regulated industry?[8] I suggest that the process of setting Medicare indemnities could be simpler than that of determining the relative fees under RBRVS. This hunch follows from the different purposes of the two systems: Whereas the RBRVS claims to replicate physicians' actual costs, the indemnity system is designed to pay some portion of what the doctor charges. To set the indemnities, Congress would have to decide how much, on average, of the doctors' charges patients should be expected to pay. This decision would be less complicated than setting prices that are supposed to measure the costs of thousands of different services.[9]

I also suggest that a considerable percentage of all Part B spending for physicians' services could be captured by a relatively small number of indemnities. Table 4-1 shows the top fifty principal diagnoses for Medicare-allowed charges by physicians and suppliers in 2002.

The top fifty diagnoses accounted for 54 percent of the $81 billion of Medicare-allowed charges by physicians and suppliers in 2002. In comparison, the top fifty "HCPCS" codes, representing the types of services performed, accounted for 47 percent of allowed charges (Centers for Medicare and Medicaid Services 2006, table 64). Thus, the types of illness represented in the Medicare population appear to be somewhat more concentrated than the types of services provided. This should make it easier to focus on setting the indemnity payments—in contrast to the difficulty of trying to determine the cost of each service provided.

Another way of looking at this issue is to examine the causes of death of Medicare beneficiaries (although this information is somewhat dated). Analyzing a six-year file of Medicare use and cost data linked to death certificates, Riley and Lubitz (1989) found that almost 70 percent of the 1.27 million Medicare beneficiaries over age sixty-five who died in 1979 died from three major causes: heart disease (40.9 percent), cancer (18.0 percent), and stroke (10.5 percent). During the year prior to death, these beneficiaries spent 3.38, 6.62, and 3.68 times as much, respectively, as the average aged Medicare enrollee.[10] Therefore, from this perspective as well, health-care spending in the Medicare population is concentrated on

TABLE 4-1

TOP FIFTY PRINCIPAL DIAGNOSES FOR MEDICARE-ALLOWED
CHARGES BY PHYSICIANS AND SUPPLIERS, 2002

Description of illness	ICD-9-CM code	$ million allowed charges
Malignant neoplasm of colon	153	$488
Malignant neoplasm of trachea, bronchus, and lung	162	$1,096
Other malignant neoplasm of skin	173	$909
Malignant neoplasm of female breast	174	$958
Malignant neoplasm of prostate	185	$1,999
Thyroiditis	244	$252
Diabetes mellitus	250	$2,542
Disorders of lipoid metabolism	272	$682
Disorders of fluid, electrolyte, and acid-base balance	276	$286
Other and unspecified anemias	285	$1,084
Schizophrenic disorders	295	$323
Affective psychoses	296	$711
Other retinal disorders	362	$1,055
Glaucoma	365	$844
Cataract	366	$3,262
Essential hypertension	401	$1,924
Acute myocardial infarction	410	$332
Other acute and subacute forms of ischemic heart disease	411	$362
Angina pectoris	413	$428
Other forms of chronic ischemic heart disease	414	$2,546
Other diseases of endocardium	424	$617
Cardiac dysrhythmias	427	$1,419
Heart failure	428	$1,457
Ill-defined descriptions and complications of heart disease	429	$189

continued on the next page

continued from page 41

Acute, but ill-defined, cerebrovascular disease	436	$733
Acute bronchitis and bronchiolitis	466	$203
Allergic rhinitis	477	$213
Pneumonia, organism undefined	486	$506
Asthma	493	$430
Other diseases of lung	518	$782
Chronic renal failure	585	$1,392
Calculus of kidney and ureter	592	$130
Other disorders of urethra and urinary tract	599	$551
Hyperplasia of prostate	600	$382
Other dermatoses	702	$683
Chronic ulcer of skin	707	$519
Rheumatoid arthritis and other inflammatory polyarthropathies	714	$557
Osteoarthrosis and allied disorders	715	$1,850
Other and unspecified arthropathies	716	$230
Other and unspecified disorders of joint	719	$844
Other and unspecified disorders of back	724	$1,416
Peripheral enthesopathies and allied syndromes	726	$401
Other disorders of soft tissues	729	$443
Nonallopathic lesions, not elsewhere classified	739	$417
General symptoms	780	$1,993
Symptoms involving respiratory systems/ other chest symptoms	786	$2,662
Symptoms involving digestive system	787	$741
Symptoms involving urinary system	788	$389
Other ill-defined and unknown causes of morbidity and mortality	799	$273
Fracture of neck or femur	820	$507
Total top fifty diagnoses		**$45,012**

Source: Centers for Medicare and Medicaid Services 2006, table 63.
Note: ICD-9-CM is a classification system of morbidity data that is used for indexing medical records, medical care review, and basic health statistics. The three-digit codes shown here could be further subdivided to a fourth decimal place for finer detail.

a fairly small number of diseases. Of course, there can be wide variation in the cost of an illness depending on severity or disease stage, so these data are not meant to be definitive.

How Much Risk Is There, and How Much Is Acceptable? The primary advantage of indemnity payments is that Medicare patients will face the full marginal cost of consuming expensive medical care. The primary drawback is that patients, especially those with low incomes, could be exposed to a substantial risk that the cost of their treatment will greatly exceed the indemnity. This point was made by David Cutler (2002, 36), who wrote,

> If there is variability in disease severity within indemnity groups which cannot be contracted on—for example variation in the particular intervention or in recovery time—a fixed indemnity payment still exposes the individual to substantial risk. Exposure to this risk involves a welfare loss. As medical technology has become more complex and optimal treatments have become more differentiated, the ability to adequately design such policies has declined.

To illustrate this problem, imagine that your automobile has been damaged, and the insurance adjuster presented this report to you: "The average cost of your repair is $1,000, but it could cost anywhere between $200 and $10,000. Here's your check for $1,000. Good luck." Auto insurance with this amount of risk to the policyholder wouldn't last long in the marketplace. Why should we expect that medical indemnity insurance, where the "repair" can cost hundreds of thousands of dollars, will fare any better?

Before proceeding, we need to distinguish between "unavoidable" and "avoidable" medical expenses. Part of the reason the cost of the auto repair could vary so much is that some policyholders may install unnecessarily expensive parts. The decision to spend $10,000 might be avoidable in the sense that a perfectly decent repair could be done for $2,000. The difference between $10,000

TABLE 4-2

INITIAL TREATMENT COSTS FOR CANCER IN ELDERLY MEDICARE
BENEFICIARIES AND ESTIMATES OF THE COST OF RISK-BEARING

Type of cancer	Number of cases	Mean cost	Standard deviation	Variance of cost	Total cost of risk-bearing
Breast	1,952	$12,141	$10,434	$108,868,356	$33,722–$44,160
Colorectal	2,563	$24,910	$14,870	$221,116,900	$68,491–$89,691
Lung	3,331	$21,351	$14,813	$219,424,969	$67,967–$89,004
Prostate	3,179	$14,361	$11,216	$125,798,656	$38,966–$51,027

SOURCES: Number of cases, mean cost, and standard deviation from Penberthy et al. (1999); risk aversion from Marquis and Holmer (1986); variance of cost and total cost of risk-bearing from author's calculations.

and $2,000 represents avoidable expenses. Unfortunately, neither the measures of central tendency nor the measure of risk in reported medical expenditure data distinguish between avoidable and unavoidable expenses. Therefore, reported medical expenditure data will overestimate the actual risk to which patients are exposed, but the size of that overestimate is unknown.

With this caveat in mind, Lynne Penberthy and colleagues (1999) reported on the initial treatment costs for elderly Medicare beneficiaries diagnosed with breast, colorectal, lung, or prostate cancer from 1985 through 1988. Their findings are shown in the first three columns of table 4-2.

The coefficient of variation (standard deviation divided by the mean) of cost is smallest for colorectal cancer and largest for breast cancer. The variances of cost per case, shown in the next to last column of table 4-2, are at least $100 million for all cancers. The larger the variance, the more risk the patient faces when he or she accepts an indemnity payment equal to the average cost per case.[11]

To determine how much patients would be willing to pay to avoid 100 percent of this risk, I used an estimate of risk aversion from the RAND Health Insurance Experiment (HIE). As reported by Susan Marquis and Martin Holmer (1986), patients in the HIE were willing to pay between forty-two and fifty-five cents to avoid each one thousand dollars of risk (in 1982 dollars). I converted their estimates to 1985–88 dollars, matching the period studied by Penberthy et al., and multiplied by the variances of cost per case to obtain estimates of the cost of risk-bearing shown in the last column of table 4-2.[12] According to my calculations, the cost of risk-bearing ranges from a low of $33,722 for breast cancer (using Marquis and Holmer's lower willingness-to-pay estimate) to almost $90,000 (using their higher willingness-to-pay estimate) for colorectal and lung cancers.[13]

I don't claim that these calculations are accurate down to the last dollar. Nevertheless, the message is quite clear: Patients who received an indemnity equal to the average cost of treating these common cancers would be exposed to unacceptably high risk that their treatment cost would substantially exceed the indemnity payment. This means that a system of pure indemnity payments is not likely to be viable for these types of cancer.[14]

This brings us back to Pauly's 1971 article. For some conditions that are "relatively straightforward" (58), Pauly thought that pure indemnities might be feasible. For others where the range of treatment costs is quite large, such as the cancers shown above, pure indemnity insurance would need to be supplemented with a major medical policy of some type. With admirable clarity, he wrote, "A more reasonable approach might be one which combines a set indemnity with partial coverage of the risk that the excess of charges over the indemnity level will be large" (57).

There are several ways to design this mixed indemnity. One is to charge coinsurance on the excess of actual costs minus the indemnity.[15] Another, recommended by Gianfrancesco (1983), is to require a deductible before the excess charges are covered by a catastrophic insurance policy. Because the patient's ability to bear risk might vary by income, the coinsurance or deductible could be reduced or waived for lower-income patients. A third strategy is to "carve out" certain services that are part of the treatment bundle and continue to reimburse these through traditional health insurance. The carved-out services could be those that comprise a minimum treatment plan for the condition, or those that are especially risky, such as emergency hospitalizations.

An insurance policy with first-dollar indemnity coverage, followed by a deductible and catastrophic coverage after the deductible is met, sounds like the "donut hole" in Medicare Part D drug coverage, but it is not.[16] All of the money in the indemnity has a marginal opportunity cost equal to that of cash, because the patient can use the indemnity to buy nonmedical goods. The deductible that follows the indemnity also has an opportunity cost equal to that of cash. Therefore, all of the indemnity plus the deductible has a full cash value to the consumer. This means that a mixed policy with a $10,000 indemnity followed by a $5,000 deductible is equivalent to a policy with a $15,000 deductible. Patients have strong incentives to use the first $15,000 of medical expenses carefully, as they would if they were spending their own money. In contrast, insurance coverage in Medicare Part D after paying a $275 deductible does not provide strong incentives for patients to be careful consumers of prescription drugs.

A single indemnity payment covering expected lifetime treatment costs would be very risky for patients with chronic conditions. In such cases, the risk could be lessened by paying a series of indemnities in annual installments corresponding to the expected annual costs of maintenance care, possibly supplemented with major medical insurance as noted above.

Feigenbaum (1992) proposed a different solution to the risk-bearing problem that does not rely on mixed indemnities. According to her recommendations, "Insurers would guarantee that their settlement would be accepted as payment in full by contracted preferred providers" (3). While interesting, this proposal has several weaknesses. First, it seems to have been borrowed from the analogy with auto repair shops, but there is an important difference between "auto repair" and "people repair." The auto repair shop has a good idea how much it will cost to fix and repaint a bumper—there is not much risk in accepting this job. But physicians may not know how much it will cost to treat a case of cervical cancer—the risk of accepting this job is substantial. Simply transferring that risk from patients to physicians does not eliminate it, although physicians might be able to pool the risk if they treat many patients with the same indemnified diagnosis. A second problem with Feigenbaum's proposal is that it resembles the physician DRGs discussed earlier. Dividing the indemnity among multiple providers is not a costless transaction.

More important, this proposal does not really turn decision-making power over to patients. Some patients might not want to contract with a single provider for their treatment, and others might not want to purchase standard medical treatment at all. The point of an indemnity is to let patients manage their health care with dollars that have other uses on the margin.

On the other hand, Feigenbaum's proposal would be useful for patients who want to contract for a standard treatment at a set price. She specified that physicians who accept the indemnity payment in full would be "preferred," which implies that this decision would be voluntary on the part of the physician, rather than mandated by the Medicare program. This means that it could be one option among several available to patients.

Costly Verification. I have mentioned that verifying the occurrence of the event covered by the indemnity could be a significant problem. How can an indemnity be designed to overcome it? One approach discussed in the literature (Kaplow 1994) is to use a multistage verification process. The first stage would be a relatively cheap and reliable determination whether the patient has suffered the condition at all. This could be based on a verified diagnosis of diabetes in a medical record, for example. The indemnity awarded at this initial stage should be relatively small. However, patients should have the right to appeal the initial determination. As explained by Kaplow (148), "When there is an appeal, individuals should receive higher payments only if their demonstrated loss exceeds the initial award by a nontrivial, and perhaps substantial, amount, so as to avoid what otherwise would be an excessive incentive to appeal claims." In the context of medical indemnities, the appeal could be based on the severity of the disease or condition. Essentially, this is a risk-adjusted indemnity. Similar determinations already are used to establish the severity of long-term care needs, although severity-adjusted payments are made to the nursing home, not directly to the patient, as would be done with an indemnity.

Must the Indemnity Be Spent on Medical Care? Recall that "pure" indemnities are fixed amounts of money paid to an individual after the occurrence of a well-defined event. After the individual receives the payment, he or she is free to spend it on a repair or not. Should the same principle be followed for Medicare indemnities?

Feigenbaum (1992) discussed this question in detail. While she generally favored letting patients decide how to spend their money,[17] she allowed that "there are circumstances when it may be appropriate to demand that an insurance settlement be dedicated in its entirety to medical care" (5). The list of such instances includes treatment for infectious diseases that have serious public health consequences, and settlements made on behalf of minors and mentally incompetent patients. These examples involve either substantial externalities where the government already uses its coercive power to force individuals to use medical care (such as vaccinations) or situations where the decision-maker is presumed unable to exercise an informed, independent decision regarding medical treatment.

What about compelling informed adults to use medical care when the benefits of treatment are purely private? Feigenbaum suggested that terminally ill patients might "be required to obtain hospice coverage" (5).[18] She did not explain, however, why rational, terminally ill adults should be required to use hospice services if they expressly wished not to.

At least three possible arguments can be made for Feigenbaum's position that a minimum level of coverage should be required. All of them require that we lay aside the economist's usual advice that people should be allowed to do as they wish with an insurance settlement. The first argument is that public medical programs, by their very nature, involve an externality that arises because the program transfers money to "recipients" from "donors" who have preferences regarding how the money should be spent. If recipients were free to use the money as they wished, the donors' utility would be lower than if the recipients had to spend some of the money on medical care. Therefore, letting recipients spend the money any way they wish is not optimal for society as a whole.[19] This argument is most obvious with Medicaid, which transfers money from taxpayers to poor and elderly recipients who meet federal and state requirements for subsidized medical assistance. Medicare also is financed by taxpayers who subsidize medical benefits for the elderly and some disabled beneficiaries. Political support for these programs might be reduced substantially if beneficiaries were free to spend their indemnities on nonmedical goods.

The second argument for requiring the indemnity to be spent on medical care is that contracts in which patients eschewed any use of medical care might not be enforceable. Imagine that a terminally ill patient who refused all forms of medical care, including hospice care, and spent her indemnity on other goods, collapses at the door of a hospital. Would she be turned away? It is difficult to imagine that she would be denied access to all medical care. Quite possibly, she would be treated and referred to a hospice, so society would wind up paying twice—once for the indemnity and again for the charity hospice care.

Can patients be prevented from spending their money on other goods and then seeking charity care? Clark Havighurst (1995) has proposed that patients and health plans, such as Medicare, be permitted to write binding *ex ante* contracts that specify the rights and responsibilities of each party. In this case, the beneficiary could be required to sign a contract stating that he or she will not seek charity care for the condition that was indemnified. I feel uneasy about dismissing Havighurst's position, but I doubt that society would have the stomach to enforce such contracts. Let me explain why.

Havighurst placed most of the blame for the lack of contracts that bind consumers to follow economizing health-care choices on the courts. For example, he wrote that judges are "reluctant to deny coverage to any patient with a sympathy-inspiring claim" (Havighurst 1995, 22). Such antipathy on the part of courts creates a chilling effect on contract drafters. Nevertheless, Havighurst believed that health plans could use three contracting strategies to authorize rational economizing in the provision of health care. First, they could attempt to specify more clearly the particular services or circumstances in which subscribers do not deem the marginal benefits of medical treatment to exceed the marginal cost. Second, in cases where particular decisions are disputed, the dispute could be settled by an independent third party. Third, the plan could take advantage of clinical guidelines to specify when care is not warranted. Havighurst believed that "courts would generally respect contracts of the sort proposed" (308).

I am much less sanguine about the enforceability of such contracts, not because of antipathy of the courts, but because of the public opprobrium that would be heaped on a health plan (including Medicare) that denied medical care after the fact, even if the patient had agreed a priori to such denial. In other words, Havighurst did not foresee the backlash against managed care that was looming on the horizon in the mid-1990s, centering on the fear that patients in managed-care plans would not receive the services they needed when they were sick. In a survey of managed-care enrollees (Blendon et al. 1998), a majority (55 percent) said they were at least "somewhat worried" that if they were sick, their health plan would be more concerned about saving money than about what was the best medical treatment; only 34 percent of those with traditional health insurance felt this way. Americans' worst fear about managed care is that their plans won't take care of them when they are sick. Like it or not, the public perception of managed care is driven by "outlier" events— patients who died or were severely injured after their health plan denied coverage for a certain treatment. Such extremely negative perceptions would make unacceptably high the penalties for health-care plans that would try to write economizing contracts.

Short of discovering a mechanism that would give patients incentive to purchase a minimal amount of medical care, I think that the Medicare indemnity would have to specify a minimum treatment plan for at least some cases, one of them being Feigenbaum's example of terminal illness in which the beneficiary would be required to use hospice care.[20]

Another approach to solving this problem would be to require proof of the patient's ability to pay out of pocket before issuing the indemnity. For example, only patients with assets above a certain minimum level might be allowed to "cash in" the indemnity. This approach has two drawbacks. One is political—it would create the impression that only the rich have this privilege; the other is that it makes little sense to allow patients to cash in the indemnity while restricting an equal amount of their other assets.

The third reason for restricting the indemnity to medical-care spending is that it would reduce the potential for fraud and abuse. Of Medicare beneficiaries, 78 percent have at least one chronic medical condition, and half have three or more (Anderson 2002). These individuals account for almost 90 percent of total Medicare spending. Putting the problem quite simply, if they were indemnified for their chronic conditions but could spend the money any way they wanted, being diagnosed with a chronic condition could trigger large and quasi-permanent annuity payments. The incentives for patients and physicians to make false claims would be overwhelming. These incentives could be reduced by restricting the indemnity to be spent on medical care.

Before leaving this question, I should note that I don't think unrestricted indemnity payments should be outside the bounds of the debate over Medicare reform. In 1996, a demonstration of unrestricted indemnities actually was undertaken at the Medical College of Virginia in Richmond. In this experiment, terminally ill cancer patients were randomly assigned to traditional fee-for-service care or to an indemnity where they received $18,000 to spend on anything they wanted. The $18,000 figure was selected because it represented the average cost of six months of chemotherapy. If patients randomized to the indemnity group wanted chemotherapy, they had to pay for it from the $18,000. According to Thomas Smith, MD, director of cancer education at the Massey Cancer Center at MCV, "Our main concern is how to get patients involved in their own medical decisions at the end of life" (Jenks 1996, 865). Unfortunately, as related by Graboyes (2000, 7), "For regulatory and other reasons, the peer group offered this option was small and produced fewer results than had been hoped for." Consequently, the findings from this interesting and potentially pathbreaking study were never published.

To learn more about the problems encountered by the study, I contacted Karen Swisher, professor of health law and bioethics at the Medical College of Virginia and principal investigator of "Effects of Case Management Alternatives on the Cost of Care and Quality of Life for End Stage Non-Small Cell Lung Cancer Patients," sponsored by Trigon Blue Cross/Blue Shield of Virginia. According to Swisher, community physicians in Richmond wanted to be paid to recruit patients for the study; the investigators did not want to pay, so they relied on their faculty colleagues at MCV to recruit patients. Unfortunately, these salaried physicians were more interested in recruiting patients into their own research studies than assisting in this one. Ultimately, only one patient was enrolled in the indemnity plan. The patient used the money to buy a beach house, but demanded more aggressive care when the illness progressed. The insurance plan that covered this patient relented, and the patient got the aggressive care. This sample, albeit of one patient, illustrates the problem of enforcing contracts with patients to forgo medical care—even if patients agree to these contracts a priori.

In addition to the recruitment problem, this study was not a trial of pure indemnities because the only medical services that were carved out of the patient's insurance policy were those considered by the investigators to be "futile"—that is, medical care that purported to cure or extend the life of the terminally ill subject. Medical care for all conditions not related to the patient's cancer, as well as palliative care (such as pain relief), were covered. Therefore, this experiment could be considered to be a mixture of an indemnity and a regular medical insurance policy.

5

Medicare Supplementary Insurance Must Go

For my proposal—or any proposal that uses prices to signal patients' preferences—to work, Medicare needs to impose some patient cost-sharing. As I discussed in chapter 2, private Medicare supplementary insurance removes cost-sharing for as many as 78 percent of all elderly and disabled Medicare beneficiaries. The effect of this price distortion has been documented by numerous studies. Sandra Christensen, Stephen Long, and James Rodgers (1987) reported that Medicare supplements were associated with a 23.8 percent increase in spending for Medicare Part A and 24.3 percent for Part B.

Part of this increase in Medicare spending could be due to "adverse selection," meaning that the individuals who purchase Medigap policies are sicker than those without Medigap. At first glance, this seems unlikely, because the elderly who purchase Medigap policies are younger and in better self-assessed health than those without supplements (Ettner 1997). These findings do not, however, rule out the possibility that these individuals have unmeasured characteristics that are associated with greater need for medical care. Two studies have attempted to control for unmeasured selection into Medigap. First, Susan Ettner (1997) examined spending differences between elderly individuals without Medigap and those who got Medigap insurance through an employer. She argued that getting Medigap through an employer reduces the importance of individual selection. Her findings indicated that persons with "basic" Medigap coverage (that is, policies that do not cover prescription drugs or nursing home care) spent $281 more in Medicare-reimbursed services in 1991 than those without Medigap. Policies with either prescription drugs or nursing home care or both were associated with $760 of additional Medicare reimbursement.

Second, Adam Atherly used an econometric technique to model the choice of both individual and employer-provided Medigap plans. After correcting for unobserved selection into these policies, Atherly found that "individual supplemental plans without prescription drugs increased Medicare expenditures by $914 annually, while those with drugs increased Medicare expenditures by $491. Employer policies also increased Medicare expenditures ($207 [1995 dollars] without drug coverage and $447 with drug coverage). Reviewing the literature, Atherly concluded, "The only consistent finding across the studies is that supplemental insurance policies are associated with increased expenditures" (2002, 137, 139).

Based on these results, it is clear that Medigap insurance removes price as a factor influencing the demand for medical care among elderly policyholders. Furthermore, once the Medigap policy has fulfilled Medicare's cost-sharing requirements, approximately 80 percent of the additional physicians' expenses and as much as 100 percent of the additional hospital expenses are paid by Medicare. According to Frech (1999, 115), "The most important immediate reform of Medicare would be to prohibit or discourage Medigap policies that fill in Medicare's cost-sharing." Therefore, at long last, let's get rid of private Medicare supplements.

The 2003 Medicare Modernization Act (Public Law 108-173) took a giant step in this direction by prohibiting Medigap plans (except those purchased through an employer group) from selling coverage supplementing the Medicare Part D drug benefit. As of January 1, 2006, no new "Medigap Rx policy" could be sold, issued, or renewed to Part D enrollees. This applied to individuals who were not enrolled, as well, except that continuation was permitted for those who purchased a Medigap Rx policy prior to that date.

In an earlier analysis, Bryan Dowd, Jon Christianson, and I (1996) explained several ways to get rid of Medigap. One would be to end the current federal subsidy of Medigap premiums. Each time a patient with Medigap uses a covered Medicare service, approximately 80 percent of the cost after the statutory deductible for Part

B and 100 percent of the cost after the deductible for Part A is paid by Medicare, leaving the Medigap plan to pay only the remaining amount. We suggested that Medigap premiums could be taxed by an amount equal to the effect of the Medigap policy on basic Medicare fee-for-service costs.

A second way to end the subsidy would be to end Medigap insurance itself by requiring Medigap insurers to become comprehensive health plans that take financial responsibility for covering the full cost of basic Medicare benefits, just like Medicare HMOs. Those insurers could then sell any package of supplementary benefits they wished, at whatever premium the market would pay, but they would be responsible for 100 percent of the costs. This analysis still is relevant.

It might be argued that Medigap insurance would disappear on its own if we moved to a Medicare indemnity system because there would be no demand for covering deductibles and coinsurance if these were replaced by an indemnity. Patients might demand supplemental insurance, however, to cover the difference between the indemnity and their treatment costs under a "worst case" scenario (see chapter 4 on management of risk under an annuity system). If a patient who purchased such a policy experienced a less-serious illness, he or she might decide to spend the whole indemnity, rather than cashing part of it, in order to qualify for additional subsidized spending under the supplementary policy. Any time we let the supplementary policy cover the same condition that is covered by the primary insurer, the supplement will create perverse incentives for overspending. Thus, while the demand for supplementary insurance to cover "front-end" expenses would presumably disappear under an indemnity system, the existence of supplementary insurance as secondary payer would continue to be a problem unless steps such as those outlined above were taken.

6

Physician Market Power and Indemnities

In this chapter I will describe another barrier to the successful implementation of indemnities: Physicians have market power to charge prices higher than their marginal costs. Without correcting this problem, patients would be overmatched by providers in the marketplace. I argue, however, that three steps can be taken to make the market more competitive.

Evidence of Market Power

One objection certain to be raised against Medicare indemnities is that patients, like sheep turned loose amid a pack of wolves, would be hopelessly overmatched by providers in the marketplace for Part B services. As Kathryn Langwell put it, "Proponents of direct price controls believe that the market for health services is irretrievably flawed" (1993, 5). Karen Davis and Sara Collins, for example, remarked in a recent article that "Medicare's long-term relative success in holding down spending is partly a result of its structured payment systems and regulatory controls" (2005–6, 57). According to proponents of this view, patients would wind up paying far more for Medicare Part B services under an indemnity program than they do with the current system of price controls.

I would like to discuss this objection from two different perspectives. First, is the market for physicians' services competitive? Second, if it is not competitive, what should we do about it?

Plenty of evidence shows that while the market for physicians' services does not fit the model of pure monopoly, it is far from competitive. This evidence was summarized nicely by Frech (1996), who drew the following contrast: If the market were perfectly competitive, an individual physician who raised his or her price by a small amount would lose 100 percent of his or her patients to other physicians; but if each physician were a pure monopolist, the same price increase would result in no loss of patients to other physicians (the only loss of patients experienced by a pure monopolist would occur because some patients would make fewer visits). These contrasting cases can be framed in terms of the "price elasticity of demand," which measures the percentage change in quantity demanded divided by a 1 percent change in price. Individual physicians in a perfectly competitive market would face infinitely elastic demand curves, while pure monopolists would face demand curves that have the same price elasticity as the total market demand for physicians' services.

The RAND Health Insurance Experiment (Newhouse et al. 1993) found that the elasticity of demand for outpatient visits to physicians and other health providers was approximately –.33 (that is, a 1 percent increase in price was associated with a .33 percent decrease in quantity demanded).[1] Thus, if individual physicians were pure monopolists, each would have faced a demand curve with a price elasticity of –.33.

Frech (1996) reviewed the results of studies that have estimated the price elasticity of demand facing individual physicians. While the results were not uniform, in every case the price elasticity was much greater in absolute value than –.33. "Except for the elderly with comprehensive insurance, the estimates from all sources range from –1.75 to –5.2. For primary care physicians, the range of directly estimated elasticities is tighter, from –1.75 to –3.32" (Frech 1996, 79).

These findings reject the model of pure monopoly, but they also suggest that the market for physicians' services is far from competitive. According to economic theory, profit-maximizing physicians facing these demand conditions could mark up their prices anywhere between 19 percent and 57 percent above their marginal costs.[2] Markups of this size would be considered very substantial by antitrust agencies (U.S. Department of Justice and Federal Trade

Commission 1997), which look upon 5 percent markups as evidence of sellers' market power.

More recently, Barry Selden, Chulho Jung, and Roberto Cavazos (1998) used an econometric technique to measure the extent of monopoly power in the market for physicians' services. The idea behind their technique is quite simple. When the demand curve for any product rotates around the point where it crosses the marginal cost curve, price and quantity will not change in a competitive market. If the market is a monopoly, however, and the demand curve becomes steeper (that is, less elastic), price will increase. The authors measured the amount by which the price of physicians' services increases when the demand curve becomes steeper, and they concluded from these measurements that the price elasticity of demand was –2.96. Interestingly, this was close to the midpoint of the range of earlier estimates reviewed by Frech. Selden, Jung, and Cavazos (1998, 799) concluded that physicians have "nontrivial" market power, which "suggests that conventional policy tools could reduce costs in this market."

Subjective and spotty, but nevertheless suggestive, evidence also indicates that physicians' market power is on the rise vis-à-vis private health plans. Among other bits of evidence, the proportion of physicians who do not contract with any managed-care plan rose from 9.2 percent in 2000–2001 to 11.5 percent in 2004–5 (O'Malley and Reschovsky 2006). Among physicians with such contracts, the use of capitation, or fixed monthly payments for each patient regardless of the amount of care provided, was declining (Strunk and Reschovsky 2002).[3] Finally, case studies of contract negotiations between managed-care plans and health-care providers have indicated "a growing recognition by plans that the balance of power now clearly favors providers" (White, Hurley, and Strunk 2004, 1). Physicians and hospital systems have consolidated to achieve negotiating leverage with health plans.

In sum, the current market for physicians' services is not competitive, and subjective evidence indicates that physicians' market power vis-à-vis private health plans is increasing. What should we do about this mess?

The regulatory response would reduce the overall level of Medicare fees. But this does not solve the problem of market power, and, given the limitations on balance billing, most economic models predict that lower fees eventually would squeeze Medicare patients out of the market because physicians would supply more services to more remunerative private patients. Sooner or later, we would expect to see signs of lower Medicare quality (for example, shorter visits and longer waiting times to get appointments) and more physicians refusing to accept Medicare patients. These predictions are consistent with evidence that physicians' willingness to accept Medicare assignment is highly related to reimbursement levels. In an early study, for example, Lynn Paringer (1980) found that a 1 percent reduction in reimbursement levels would result in a 0.5–1.5 percent reduction in the assignment rate, controlling for other factors. Likewise, Janet Mitchell and Jerry Cromwell (1982) found that a 1 percent decrease in the Medicare prevailing charge reduced assignment by 1.47 percent.

More recently, Kurt Gillis and David Lee (1997) examined the importance of reimbursement and other factors in determining physicians' willingness to accept new Medicare patients. Among general and family practitioners, they found that the fee index had a large positive effect, with a 10 percent increase in the index associated with an increase of roughly five percentage points in the likelihood of accepting all new Medicare patients. The fee level did not, however, have a significant effect on general internists' willingness to accept new Medicare patients. The authors noted several possible explanations for this finding, such as the lack of variation in the fee index for internists and the importance of Medicare revenue for this specialty, with the implication that an internist may have difficulty operating a viable practice without accepting new Medicare patients.

Regarding quality of services, MedPAC's official position is that the level of payments to physicians is positively related to their ability to furnish high-quality services (Medicare Payment Advisory Commission 2003b). Another problem with reducing Medicare fees is that Medicare doesn't exist in a vacuum. Virtually all types of medical care used by Medicare beneficiaries, with the possible exception of treatment for end-stage renal disease, are also used by individuals with private insurance. My colleagues and I (Dowd et al., 2006–7) analyzed the problems that arise when there are multiple payers (for example, Medicare and private insurance) and a monopolistic provider. The monopolist will supply services to each payer so that the marginal revenue from privately insured patients equals the Medicare fee and the marginal cost of services, assuming that marginal costs are the same in both markets. Now suppose that Medicare used its buying power to determine the fees it pays to doctors. Even if Medicare set the right price (that is, one that resulted in physicians supplying the quantity of services that Medicare wanted to buy), the private price would exceed the marginal cost because of monopoly power in the private insurance market. Consequently, Medicare cannot use its buying power to solve the problem of providers' market power when there are multiple payers in the market.

Three Steps toward a Competitive Market

It would take three steps to make Medicare more competitive: First, patients must have good information about prices and quality of physicians; second, they must have an incentive to act on that information; and, third, providers must act as price-takers and must not be able to collude to set prices for their services.

A great deal has been written about consumer information in health-care markets, much of it focusing on how to present information in a way that patients understand and trust (see Lubalin and Harris-Kojetin 1999 for a review of the literature). Presenting good information on price and quality would, unquestionably, be a challenge to a Medicare indemnity program. But isn't information a challenge in today's price-controlled world as well? I would argue that the answer is yes.

Some might say that consumers don't need good information in today's price-controlled world because 99 percent of charges allowed by Medicare are taken on assignment. Consequently, even if patients had some cost-sharing in their Medicare insurance policies, they would pay the same out-of-pocket prices regardless of their choices of providers. This argument is wrong for several reasons. First, it applies only to the price of each service, not the price of the set of services comprising the treatment for a given condition. Some providers might treat the condition more intensively than others, leading to more coinsurance or copayments for the patient.

More important is that controlled prices can hide differences in quality among physicians. Some years ago, Frank Sloan and I (Feldman and Sloan 1989) analyzed how price controls work in a market where physicians are monopolists and their services vary in two dimensions—quantity and quality. As a reference point, we began by fixing quality. The monopolist would produce too little of the good and sell it at a profit. A regulatory agency, however, could control the monopolist's price at the competitive level, leading to the socially optimal outcome. Now let quality vary as well. Because the regulator has only one instrument (price) to hit two targets (quality and quantity), it is forced to make tradeoffs. Specifically, if the regulator forces the monopolist to cut price in order to increase quantity, quality will fall. For example, doctors may cut their visit lengths and boost the number of visits or other billable services such as laboratory tests. If price is cut to the level where quantity is just right, quality will be too low.

Now imagine that different physicians face different demand and cost conditions. Then, at the "right" price for quantity, quality may be much too low for physician A, somewhat too low for B, and so forth. The patient may know that he or she will pay the same out-of-pocket price to both physicians (because they both accept assignment), but the quality of care may vary significantly. In fact, the price controls will cause quality to vary among physicians. This means that the current regulatory approach without good information on quality is just as flawed, and possibly more so, than a Medicare indemnity system without good information.

Information on quality matters to patients, even in today's Medicare program, with its flawed (or nonexistent) price signals. On March 3, 2006, the *New York Times* reported an extraordinary news story about Medicare patients. Several years ago, Medicare approved a popular but risky surgical procedure for patients with advanced emphysema. Many experts predicted that tens of thousands of patients would sign up for the operation, which can cost more than $50,000, including months of rehabilitation. Instead, after seeing the results of a clinical trial that showed no lengthening of life for most patients and a surgical mortality of nearly 10 percent, patients and the doctors who referred them to surgeons stayed away in droves. From January 2004 through September 2005, only 458 Medicare patients filed claims for the surgery, at a total cost of less than $10.5 million to Medicare. The *Times* (Kolata 2006) quoted Scott Ramsey, MD, an internist and health economist at the University of Washington, as saying, "You could have knocked me over with a feather." The significance of this news story is that Medicare patients will pay attention to information on quality. Even though many of them could have signed up for the surgical procedure without any out-of-pocket cost-sharing, few did so.

Of the three steps toward a competitive market, the second— creating incentives to act on information—is the easiest to implement, since indemnities would have the same value to beneficiaries as cash (provided that the unused portion could be cashed in). In fact, the creation of Medicare indemnities might lead to a "virtuous cycle," in which less and less antitrust enforcement would be needed to maintain competition. (As explained in chapter 5, Medicare supplementary insurance would also have to be eliminated so Medicare patients would pay the full market price of Medicare Part B services.)

The third step—ensuring that providers do not have market power—requires strong enforcement of the antitrust laws. I would like to rely on Deborah Haas-Wilson's analysis of the role of antitrust in health care. She writes, "Enforcement of the antitrust laws . . . is a potent weapon against anticompetitive behavior (collusion or consolidation in order to raise prices) on the part of hospitals, physician organizations, and insurers" (2003, 5). Antitrust enforcement can also be seen as a signal that such behavior will not be tolerated, so it acts as a deterrent by attaching a legal risk to anticompetitive acts.

Haas-Wilson mentioned several instances in which antitrust enforcement has been brought to bear against physicians. In one case, the U.S. Federal Trade Commission charged a physicians' independent practice association (IPA) in Jacksonville, Florida, with conspiring to fix the prices its members charged to third-party payers. An IPA is an association of independent physicians formed for the purpose of integrating the clinical practices of its members. The FTC alleged, however, that the main purpose of the Jacksonville IPA was to facilitate price agreements among its members without their practices being integrated. The physicians agreed to dissolve the IPA, not to deal collectively with third-party payers, and not to fix prices. In another case, the FTC charged a corporation of ten surgeons in Broward County, Florida, with conspiring to fix fees they charged at trauma centers in two local hospitals. This case also resulted in an agreement to dissolve the physicians' corporation.

The FTC generally has a good record in its efforts to stop illegal price-fixing by physicians. My recommendation is in agreement with Haas-Wilson's: "Competitive markets are in the public interest in most cases, and in order to maintain this healthy competition, it is essential to have consistent and careful health care antitrust enforcement" (Haas-Wilson 2003, 190). Let's rely on antitrust enforcement rather than flawed regulatory approaches that merely suppress physicians' monopoly power.

As an interim step while the problem of physician market power is being addressed, beneficiaries might be able to purchase medical care through the networks of large private insurers, and even of Medicare itself, if they want. This would allow them to take advantage of these insurers' purchasing power to obtain more competitive prices.

7

Let's Give It a Try:
A Demonstration of Indemnities

Thinking about the risky surgical procedure for emphysema described in the 2006 *New York Times* article cited in the previous chapter, let's imagine that some patients who qualified for the procedure had been given a Medicare indemnity worth a fraction of its $50,000 cost, as well as good information about the costs and benefits of alternative treatments for emphysema. Would any of them have chosen the surgery? If Medicare patients with back pain—a condition for which expensive surgical treatment of questionable value is available—were given an indemnity equal to a fraction of the cost of back surgery and good information about the costs and benefits of alternative treatments, would they continue to use questionable surgical procedures at staggering rates?[1]

There is one way to discover the answers to these questions without making major changes in the Medicare payment system prior to knowing whether changes are advisable: Medicare can conduct a demonstration of indemnity payments for Part B physicians' services. The demonstration would test several critical design features of an indemnity system: what medical conditions should be covered; how the indemnity should be set; how risk should be managed; whether beneficiaries should be paid to participate in the demonstration; and whether the indemnity should be restricted. Except for the question of paying beneficiaries to participate, these questions were discussed in a more theoretical fashion in chapter 4. Here, I will offer practical suggestions for incorporating them into the demonstration.

What Medical Conditions Should Be Covered?

The choice of medical conditions to include in a demonstration of indemnities could be based on several factors. One could select conditions for which there are "traditional" but expensive treatments of questionable value. Patients with conditions of this type (for example, lower back pain) might choose medical management over surgery if they had to pay for surgery out of their own pockets. In fact, they might not choose traditional medical care at all, but instead opt for alternative or nontraditional therapies, such as chiropractic care. Another criterion for choosing a condition is that Medicare Part B spending for it should be substantial. This might be decided by setting a minimum percentage of total Part B spending for inclusion of a condition in the demonstration.

In chapter 4, however, I pointed out that conditions allowing for a large amount of personal discretion over how to spend the indemnity are likely to be difficult to verify. Healthy people might claim to have these conditions because they value for other reasons the items, such as chiropractic care, that comprise the nontraditional treatment. To test for this problem in the demonstration, Medicare might select some conditions with severe verification problems (back pain is a good candidate), and some where verification is not a serious issue, such as cancer. Comparisons could also be made of trends in the rates of claims for discretionary and nondiscretionary conditions in experimental and control sites.

It would be valuable to include, in addition, some conditions for which moderately priced and efficacious treatments are available, along with chronic conditions to test the use of indemnities paid over various time periods, such as annually. What would Medicare patients with these conditions choose if they were given indemnities?

How Should the Indemnity Be Set?

In 1983, Gianfrancesco proposed setting the indemnity by trial and error, starting at the modal expenditure associated with a given category of service under traditional insurance. Since that time, insurers, including Medicare, have become much more adept at using administrative data to calculate the average costs of insured groups. Consequently, trial and error would no longer be required to set the Medicare indemnity payments.

A more relevant problem is where to set the indemnity with reference to the average cost of care under traditional insurance. I have argued that this cost probably overstates the efficient indemnity, because some of the traditional cost is "gold-plated." For Medicare to attack this problem head-on, however, might raise objections that the indemnity demonstration is simply a disguised attempt to cut doctors' fees. Instead, as a starting point, Medicare could set the indemnity payment at the traditional level and observe how much beneficiaries were cashing in, on average. There is no efficiency loss when this occurs (because cash transfers are efficient), but Congress might decide that such an arrangement is inequitable.[2]

In chapter 4 I recommended that the indemnity payments be adjusted for local variation in medical-care prices, perhaps making use of the Medicare Geographic Practice Cost Indexes as a starting point. Since the current GPCIs might not be accurate enough to measure the cost of services that would be used under an indemnity plan, consideration should be given to including the cost of alternative medicine and home care in the geographic adjustment formula. Physicians' capacity could be another geographic source of variation. In areas where capacity is high relative to the sum of Medicare and private demand, the indemnity payment could be reduced somewhat, yet still cover the full cost of care. These factors suggest that demonstration sites could be selected based on variation in local market conditions, including input prices and the "tightness" of local supply and demand. Techniques for setting the indemnity payments could be tested in "tight" versus "loose" local markets.

How Should Risk Be Managed?

For many medical conditions, the variance of cost will exceed the amount of risk that patients can manage on their own. Partial indemnities may be appropriate for these conditions, but pure indemnities are not. In such cases, how should risk be managed? As a starting point, I recommend that Medicare undertake as part of its demonstration an up-to-date analysis of the cost of treating common medical conditions, as well as the amount of risk that patients are willing to bear. Measures of patients' willingness to bear risk should be contingent on their income and wealth.

As I discussed above, several designs could be used to construct partial indemnities. These include charging coinsurance on expenses above the indemnity and requiring a deductible above the indemnity before a major medical policy kicks in. In addition, if Pauly (1971) was right, pure indemnities could be used for "relatively straightforward" conditions. It might be advisable to test each of these designs in a demonstration. The following technical material provides specific illustrations and advice on how to manage risk.

Suppose that the probability density function of health-care expenses (x) in the population with a given medical condition is given by equation (2):

(2) $\quad \begin{aligned} & f(x) = \alpha e^{-ax}, x > 0 \\ & x = 0 \ elsewhere \end{aligned}$

This is known as an "exponential distribution," which has the property that the cumulative distribution function of expenses is:

(3) $\quad \begin{aligned} & F(x) = 1 - e^{-ax}, x > 0 \\ & F(x) = 0 \ elsewhere \end{aligned}$

The mean, variance, and coefficient of variation of this distribution are given by:

(4) $\quad \begin{aligned} & E(x) = 1/a \\ & V(x) = 1/a^2 \\ & CV(x) = (V(x))^{1/2} / E(x) = 1.0 \end{aligned}$

In other words, the variance of spending in an exponential distribution is equal to the square of its mean, and the coefficient of variation equals 1.0. A distribution of this type is "skewed to the right," with a long tail of very high-cost cases—thus it is a realistic way to describe medical-care spending in a population, and it fits the data in table 4-1 reasonably well (see chapter 4).

Now, suppose that the mean expense for a given condition is $10,000. If each eligible person were given an indemnity of this size, we could use the formulas above to calculate how many people would experience costs greater than the indemnity and how much they would have to pay out of pocket. For example, if the indemnity were set at the mean expense, then 37 percent of the eligible population would have costs that exceed the mean, and, on average, they would have to pay $10,000 out of pocket.[3] In other words, they would be exposed to a significant amount of risk.

This information could be used to design a mixed indemnity policy with a deductible. Using this example again, suppose there were a $1,000 deductible after eligible expenses exceeded the indemnity. Of the eligible population, 37 percent would have to pay something out of pocket, and 33 percent would exceed the deductible. For simplicity, assume that all 37 percent with positive out-of-pocket expenses would exceed the deductible (although this is actually an overstatement of their risk).[4] The mean out-of-pocket expense in the whole population would therefore be $370 (assuming expenses above the deductible were fully covered), and the variance of out-of-pocket expense would be $233,100.[5] Based on Marquis and Holmer's (1986) estimates of the cost of risk-bearing, we can determine that each eligible beneficiary would be willing to pay between $98 and $128 not to have a deductible. The point of the demonstration would be to test whether this cost is worth it in the sense that the value to beneficiaries of self-directing the first $10,000 of their expenses would be greater than $98–$128.

Should Beneficiaries Be Paid to Participate in the Demonstration?

Enrollees in the RAND Health Insurance Experiment were guaranteed that participation would make them no worse off than refusing to participate. This was accomplished by participation incentive payments (also known as "hold-harmless" payments) equal to the maximum loss they risked by changing from their existing coverage to the experimental plan to which they were assigned (Newhouse et al. 1993). In a demonstration of Medicare indemnities, a similar set of hold-harmless payments would maximize beneficiaries' incentives to participate and might even become part of a functioning indemnity program.

Unlike enrollees in the RAND Health Insurance Experiment, however, participants in the Medicare indemnity demonstration could not be held "absolutely harmless" against risk. To see why this is the case, imagine the worst thing that could happen to a participant. Even if the indemnity were risk-adjusted, the worst outcome would be to have expenses that far exceed the indemnity. In order to hold patients absolutely harmless against this risk, Medicare would have to pay 100 percent of the maximum possible expense. This would make it impossible to design a demonstration of indemnities because they would have to be set at the highest level of expense. In addition, a demonstration of this type would be prohibitively expensive.

Despite this difference from the HIE, participants in a demonstration of indemnities could be held "relatively harmless" by being offered a deal that should be acceptable to all of them a priori: The maximum deductible in the Medicare indemnity policy, less a risk premium calculated for each service, would never exceed the beneficiary's out-of-pocket cost for an equal amount of covered services in the traditional Medicare program. For example, in 2008, a beneficiary in traditional Medicare with $10,000 of covered services would pay a deductible of $135 and 20 percent coinsurance on the remainder, or $2,108 in all. He or she could be guaranteed that the deductible in the Medicare indemnity policy would never exceed $2,108, less a risk premium of approximately $100. This clearly is a "good deal" because it does not include any risk premium for traditional Medicare, nor does it consider the possibility that the beneficiary's coinsurance payments could greatly exceed $2,108 in traditional Medicare.

In addition to encouraging participation, a useful side effect of these hold-harmless payments is the opportunity they would provide to measure the degree of risk aversion among Medicare beneficiaries.

If the Marquis-Holmer (1986) risk premium were not large enough to achieve the target level of participation, it could be raised until the target was reached. Along the way, the degree of risk aversion for each beneficiary could be determined.

Should the Indemnity Be Restricted?

The question of whether the indemnity should be restricted is probably the most intensely ethical one to ask about indemnities. As I discussed in chapter 4, a continuum of possible answers to this question ranges from no restrictions at all to restricting the indemnity to being spent on medical care (that is, making it into a medical-care voucher). Intermediate positions would carve out certain services from the indemnity and require that these be covered by traditional Medicare. For example, patients with terminal cancer might be required to have hospice benefits. This design was used by the aborted Virginia Commonwealth University cancer indemnity trial that I discussed in chapter 4, which covered medical care for all conditions not related to the patient's cancer, as well as palliative care. As I argued previously, unrestricted indemnities would be unenforceable because society wouldn't have the stomach to refuse medical care after the fact, even if the patient had signed a voluntary, informed contract to forgo medical care. However, if policymakers can agree on a set of minimum benefits that cost less than the indemnity, on average, and if patients want to cash in the rest, then I see no reason to prevent them from doing so. Even if a demonstration accomplished nothing else, it would provide an opportunity to have an open and frank discussion about how much medical care society wishes to compel individuals to use.

Conclusion

Health economists generally agree that the goal of Medicare physician reimbursement is to simulate a perfectly functioning competitive market. Almost no one believes, however, that the current RBRVS fee schedule accomplishes that goal. Rather than undertaking meek reforms that attempt to find the elusive "just prices" for Medicare, I have proposed scrapping the Medicare physician payment system altogether and letting patients manage their own medical care with cash indemnities.

My proposal is likely to be unpopular among some segments of both the "left" and the "right." Among the left, many do not think elderly and frail patients can be trusted to make their own medical-care decisions. In response, I think that patients are the best managers of their own medical-care decisions. The Cash and Counseling Demonstration and Evaluation discussed in appendix 3 provides encouraging evidence that people with disabilities and their advocates would prefer to replace Medicare's list of covered services with a more flexible approach that lets patients choose the services they need.

Others might trust patients to spend their own money for televisions and automobiles but not for medical care, because the medical marketplace is flawed. Patients are overmatched by suppliers, particularly by physicians. There is no question that medical-care markets are flawed. The main problem is that physicians have market power to charge fees higher than their marginal costs. While it would be tempting to use Medicare's buying power to reduce fees, this approach will not address the flawed market conditions. My analysis of physicians' market power in chapter 6 would be equally valid in a world of indemnities or one in which Medicare pays physicians by a fee schedule.

Some on the right may be disappointed that my proposal does not address Medicare's financial problems. This is a deliberate omission. My proposal is intended to be equally valid whether Medicare is running a large deficit or a surplus. In addition, I am not proposing to "privatize" or eliminate Medicare, as some would recommend. Indemnities would strengthen Medicare by providing more value for the billions of dollars it spends each year on physicians' services. Finally, my proposal is not a "penny-pinching" scheme for reducing physicians' fees. I have even suggested that when physicians' capacity is high, the indemnity might exceed the cost of care, and patients could cash in the unused portion of the indemnity. This is a proposal for smarter Medicare payments. It's time to give it a try.

Appendix 1
A Model of Efficient Physician Prices

Baumgardner's defense of competition was based on the argument that the "efficient competitive equilibrium prices that RBRVS seeks to mimic will clear the market for the respective procedures" (1992, 1028). He provided an elegant statement of this idea in mathematical terms.

Imagine there are two Medicare procedures, A and B, with prices P_A and P_B. If we denote consumers' willingness to pay for services as "V" and providers' willingness to supply services as "U," the condition for efficient pricing is:

$$\text{(A1)} \quad V_A / V_B = P_A / P_B = U_A / U_B$$

Equation (A1) says that the ratio of consumers' marginal willingness to pay for services equals the ratio of relative prices, which in turn equals the ratio of physicians' marginal willingness to supply the services.[1] At the efficient prices, consumers will be indifferent between spending P_A for another unit of A or P_B for another unit of B, and providers will be indifferent between producing another unit of A and receiving P_A or producing another unit of B and receiving P_B.

The competitive equilibrium condition in the market for Medicare physicians' services can be shown by a graph whose axes measure production of services B and A.[2] The bowed line (known as the "production possibilities curve") that connects B' with A' indicates the maximum amounts of B and A that can be produced from the physician's given resources, which primarily comprise his or her practice time. The slope of the production possibilities curve indicates the

FIGURE A-1
COMPETITIVE EQUILIBRIUM IN THE MARKET
FOR MEDICARE PHYSICIANS' SERVICES

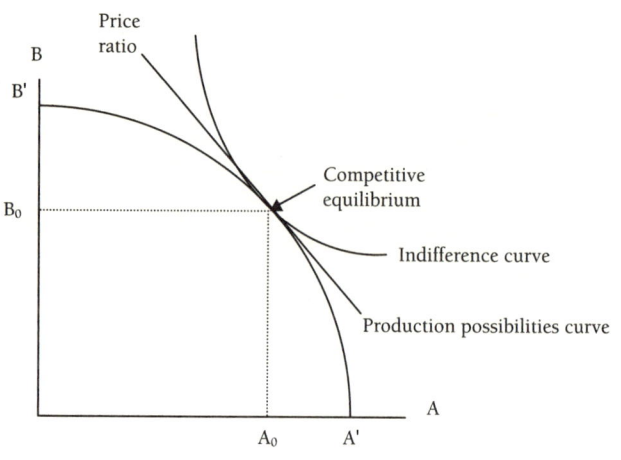

Source: Author's calculations.

marginal rate at which service B can be transformed into service A. A physician who wants to maximize his or her utility would never produce at any point inside this curve because he or she could get more income (which increases utility) by moving to the curve.

The *first fundamental theorem of welfare economics* states that a competitive market will get us to the efficient outcome described by Baumgardner without any government intervention (Rosen 2002, 38). If utility-maximizing physicians face prices shown by equation (A1), they will locate where the marginal rate of transformation between B and A is equal to the price ratio; utility-maximizing patients will locate where the price ratio is equal to the slope of an indifference curve from their consumption of B and A. Because both physicians and patients face the same prices in a competitive market, their independent decisions will lead them to point (A_0, B_0), shown as the competitive equilibrium in figure A-1.

This elegant theory breaks down when providers have market power, or when consumer demand is not fully informed, rational,

FIGURE A-2

PRICE CONTROLS BASED ON MONOPOLY RESOURCE COSTS

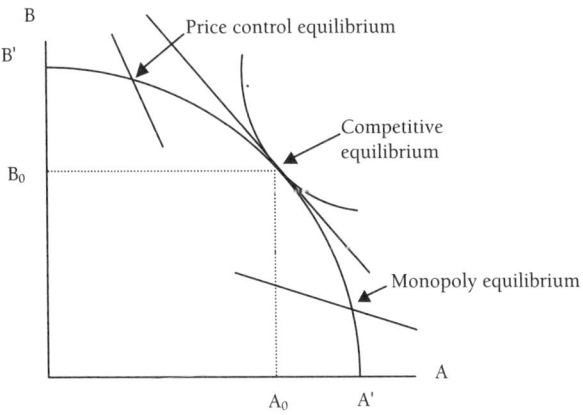

Source: Author's calculations.

or voluntary. The appeal of price controls arises because they appear to be a way to correct the market failures in Medicare. If the market is not competitive, however, the very factors that distort relative prices also distort the relative amount of work embodied in each service that forms the RBRVS.

To illustrate the problem of finding the "right" relative price (that is, the competitive equilibrium price ratio) by using price controls, I want to consider two cases: first, when beneficiaries face the market prices for services A and B but the supply side is not competitive; second, a more realistic case, when beneficiaries have supplementary insurance for service B that reduces the out-of-pocket price of that service to zero. Both cases present difficult, if not intractable, problems for finding the right prices.

Case 1. Suppose beneficiaries face the market prices for services A and B, but physicians have market power that allows them to mark up the price of B relative to the price of A. This means that the slope of the price line, P_A/P_B, becomes flatter, as shown by figure A-2.

Because the price of service B is too high compared with the competitive equilibrium, demand shifts from B toward A, which is shown by the point labeled "monopoly equilibrium" in figure A-2. Compared with the competitive equilibrium, the monopolist produces too much of service A, and too little of B.

At the monopoly equilibrium the slope of the production possibilities curve, which measures the ratio of marginal costs, changes in the opposite direction to the change in the price ratio—that is, the marginal cost of service A rises relative to that of B. Therefore, while the price of service B is too high, its marginal cost is too low. If RBRVS fees were set according to the distorted marginal costs of A and B, demand would "overshoot" the competitive equilibrium, with too little of A and too much of B being produced. This is shown in figure A-2 by the point labeled "price control equilibrium," which lies to the upper left of the competitive equilibrium point. Another way of stating this conclusion is to say that the "distortions" in prices and marginal costs move in opposite directions, with neither corresponding to the competitive equilibrium price ratio.

As Baumgardner said, "For RBRVS to get the right prices, the relative marginal utilities at the efficient quantities must be determined" (1992, 1028). Recently, my colleagues and I (Dowd et al. 2006–7) suggested how to accomplish this task. Medicare could estimate econometric models for the quantity of Medicare services in each market that would include measures of provider competition. Medicare might find the right price by predicting quantity in each market with the competition variables set to represent high levels of provider competition. Medicare could also examine market areas, identifying those that score well on measures of health outcomes and consumer satisfaction with access to and quality of physician services. More competitive markets, with less distorted prices, might score higher on these measures. I am not sure if our suggestion is practical, but it is consistent with the point made in figure A-2, that relative prices and relative marginal costs in a monopolistic market are both flawed.

Case 2. Suppose beneficiaries have insurance that insulates them from the market price of service B but does not cover service A.[3] If

FIGURE A-3
MONOPOLY EQUILIBRIUM WITH FULLY INSURED BENEFICIARIES

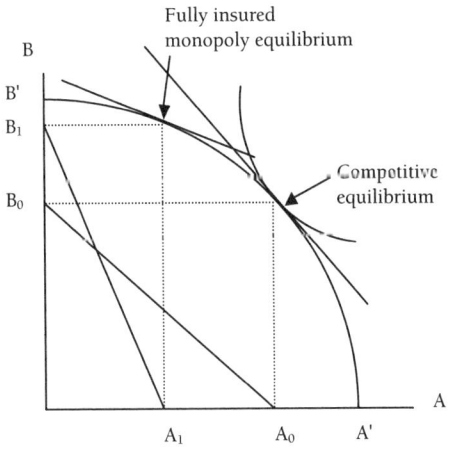

Source: Author's calculations.

the insurance policy has some cost-sharing, as was intended in Medicare, the price distortion caused by insurance might actually move the market closer to the competitive equilibrium when the insured good is supplied by a monopolist.[4] If, however, providers have monopoly power over service B and beneficiaries have a Medicare supplement that reduces the out-of-pocket price of service B to zero, both the relative price of service B and the quantity of B will be too high.[5] This outcome is shown by the monopoly equilibrium at (A_1, B_1) in figure A-3.[6] If fees are set according to either the relative price or the relative marginal cost of the services, production will be suboptimal. To move the market toward the competitive equilibrium, some mechanism must be found for basing fees on an external source of information, such as prices in more competitive markets.

Baumgardner (1992) mentioned another problem that would arise in trying to find the right prices. This is the possibility that in reporting how much "work" is involved in producing each service, physicians might report a number proportionate to the average disutility of production instead of the marginal disutility of production. The average cost of service B relative to A is shown by the slope of a line that connects the observed quantities of B and A. In competitive equilibrium, this would be the slope of line B_0A_0. At the observed point, the average cost of B rises while that of A falls—that is, B_1A_1 is steeper than B_0A_0. This means that observed average costs are not good indicators of average costs at the competitive equilibrium.

To complete this example, I want to emphasize how little can be inferred from observing the market equilibrium point. All we know is that more of service B is produced and consumed relative to A; we do not know whether the observed outcome lies to the right or left of the competitive equilibrium. Given the lack of a reference point, it is not even clear whether the relative price of B is too high.

Appendix 2
Why Did Medicare Physician Payment Reform Take So Long?

Almost no one liked Medicare's initial "customary, prevailing, and reasonable" method for paying physicians (see chapter 1). Why, then, did it take over twenty-five years from passage of the Medicare legislation to full implementation of the RBRVS payment reform? Although it is difficult to isolate the importance of individual causes, several possible explanations are worth discussing.

Medicare Part B is like an unruly younger brother to Part A—you have to take him along, but he's always getting into trouble. Medicare almost didn't have a Part B. President Lyndon B. Johnson's proposed Medicare program was a mandatory plan to cover hospital costs for the elderly. The American Medical Association opposed including physicians' services in Medicare on the grounds that it would cost too much, leading to government controls on physicians' fees (Feldstein 1999, 330). The AMA favored a means-tested program funded by general revenues. Congressional Republicans introduced a bill patterned on the AMA's proposal, calling for voluntary coverage of physicians' services.

In early 1965 the Medicare legislation languished in the U.S. Congress, with the House and Senate unable to agree on a bill. The legislative logjam was broken by Wilbur Mills, the powerful chairman of the House Ways and Means Committee. After Mills completed his review of the major health insurance bills before his committee on March 2, he made a surprising request to Wilbur Cohen, who coordinated the legislative activities related to Medicare for President Johnson. Mills took the Republican proposal for voluntary physicians' insurance, which he dubbed "Part B," and combined it with Johnson's hospital insurance plan, which he called "Part A." Part B would remain voluntary, but heavily subsidized from general revenues. Mills asked Cohen and others in the administration to draft a bill that included both parts A and B (Berkowitz 2005–6). Less than four months later, Johnson signed the Social Security Amendments of 1965 that created Medicare and Medicaid.[1]

From the beginning, Part B was less important than the more expensive Part A insurance program for hospitals. This was apparent as Congress addressed hospital payment reform in 1983 by creating the Prospective Payment System (PPS). PPS replaced cost-based reimbursement with prospective payments based on the classification of a patient's discharge into one of 470 diagnosis-related groups. Physician payment reform, in contrast, was addressed in a piecemeal fashion by patching together a series of stopgap measures, such as the 1984 payment freeze (see chapter 1).

Another factor that complicated physician payment reform was the widespread belief that relative payments were out of line, with "procedural" services being favored over "evaluation and management" services. Hsiao and colleagues were explicitly aware that "if Congress replaces the current payment system with an RBRVS-based fee schedule, there could be significant increases in the fees for some office, hospital, nursing home and consultation medical services, while some surgical fees could decrease by 10 to 35 percent" (1991, 234). The Physician Payment Review Commission also believed there were "wide payment differentials among types of procedures, localities, specialties and sites of care that cannot be explained by differences in the costs of physicians' practices" (1989, 11).

While the prospect of having "winners and losers" from implementation of the RBRVS may have rendered organized medicine unable to speak with one voice to support or oppose physician payment reform, the possibility of losing created strong opposition from the procedural specialties. On February 9, 1988, the *Wall Street Journal* reported on the "bitter battle" underway between doctors who provided cognitive services and "proceduralists," such as surgeons and radiologists. The newspaper claimed (with some justification) that the radiologists had "cut their own deal" with Congress that allowed them to have their own relative value scale, with no relation to the fees paid to other specialties (Schwartz 1988).[2] Another *Wall Street Journal* article (Ruffenach 1988) on September 9, 1988, mentioned that the medical community was "deeply divided" over the objectivity of Hsiao's study. James Moorefield, chairman of the economics commission of the American College of Radiology, was quoted as being "cynical and suspicious about the process." Predictably, the American College of Surgeons opposed the RBRVS, while the American Academy of Family Physicians supported it (Tolchin 1989).

These explanations notwithstanding, I would like to emphasize another reason Medicare physician payment reform took so long to bring about: The Reagan administration was skeptical about, if not outright opposed to, the idea of a physician fee schedule for Medicare. This fact was alluded to by the press (Ruffenach 1988; Rich 1988), but I do not believe its importance has been addressed adequately to date.

The most candid public expression of the administration's position was offered by William Roper, MD, administrator of the Health Care Financing Administration, in testimony before the House Ways and Means Committee on May 24, 1988. In his presentation, Roper attempted to draw several distinctions between physicians and hospitals that made Medicare physician payment changes far more difficult than the hospital PPS:

- There were only 475 DRGs for hospitals, compared with roughly 7,000 procedures and services for physicians.

- Whereas hospitals could average gains and losses across many cases, physicians' smaller caseloads and greater specialization would make it more difficult to average away gains and losses from changes in Medicare payment.

- The sheer number of Medicare physicians' bills was staggering.

- National physician databases did not have the level of detail and comprehensiveness of hospital databases.

Roper went on to say that no fee schedule—no matter how carefully constructed—could be expected to deal with the critical issue of "volume and intensity" of Medicare services. This phrase referred to the widespread belief that physicians would react to cuts in fees by increasing the complexity of services in order to maintain their net income. Roper asked, "Is it worth investing the lion's share of our analytical, administrative, and political resources to substitute one fee-for-service payment system for another, leaving Medicare's most important issue—increased volume and intensity—untouched?" (Roper 1988, 8).

While saying it was too early to judge the RBRVS proposal, Roper stated that capitation payments offered the greatest promise for successful long-term reform of Medicare physician payment. Less publicly, Roper had expressed this position several years earlier. In a paper prepared for the Domestic Policy Council, Roper (then a White House health policy advisor) wrote that the relative value scale was a stopgap measure and that the long-term goal was to move toward a system of capitation. Not only would capitation address the problem of volume and intensity (there would be no gain to this strategy if payment per capita were fixed), but it also would be less regulatory than a system of price controls. On October 23, 1985, the Domestic Policy Council decided against proposing physician DRGs or a national fee schedule.

It is clear that the centerpiece of the Reagan administration's health policy reform proposals was capitation. The Tax Equity and Fiscal Responsibility Act of 1982 (TEFRA) opened the door to prepaid health plans that could accept capitation payments for enrolling Medicare beneficiaries. Final regulations to implement TEFRA were published in January 1985. Health-plan capitation—not the DRG system or RBRVS—was the primary health policy accomplishment of the Reagan administration (Feldman 1988; Dowd, Feldman, and Christianson 1996).

Appendix 3
Lessons from the Cash and Counseling Demonstration and Evaluation

For years, people with disabilities and their advocates have argued that disabled individuals could improve their quality of life and/or meet their needs at less cost if they had control of the money to buy services for themselves. Starting in December 1998, some of them got a chance to do just that—and the results were promising. At that time, four states that had obtained waivers from Medicaid began to enroll volunteers in an experiment. Participants were randomly assigned to either a "cash allowance" group or a control group, thus avoiding bias that might arise from voluntary enrollment of people who would be most likely to benefit from the cash program (Mahoney, Simone, and Simon-Rusinowitz 2000).

Much has been written about the Cash and Counseling Demonstration, so I will not provide an exhaustive review. Instead, I would like to focus on several features of the program that might be relevant for a proposal to offer similar indemnity payments in Medicare.

In the first place, it is worth noting that the demonstration was a bipartisan effort. It was started by a Democratic administration and carried forward by a Republican one. Funding was provided by the Office of the Assistant Secretary for Planning and Evaluation of the U.S. Department of Health and Human Services, and the Robert Wood Johnson Foundation (RWJF). Jim Knickman, vice president in the research and evaluation team at RWJF, explained that "the idea of providing cash benefits or near-cash benefits instead of service benefits grows from the concept of consumer direction, con-sumer-directed care and patient-centered care" (Knickman 2005).

It is also noteworthy that disability advocacy organizations have been very supportive of the indemnity benefit concept. Two of them, the National Counsel on Aging and the National Association of State Units on Aging, released a set of talking points entitled, "Myths and Realities of Consumer-Directed Services for Older Persons" (Squillace and Firman 2002). Among the myths they attempted to debunk were that "older adults are not interested in consumer direction" and that "older individuals are 'vulnerable' and 'need to be protected.'" The positive reception of consumer-directed long-term care benefits by advocacy groups contrasts with the generally negative reception of consumer-directed health plans for individuals under age sixty-five by liberal organizations.

Moreover, advocates of those who care for disabled persons support the indemnity concept because it promises to pay family care-takers for their time. According to one source, the bulk of caregiving is provided by female relatives (Simon-Rusinowitz, Mahoney, and Benjamin 1998), whose ability to be self-supporting is limited by time away from the workforce. The burden of unpaid family care-giving is especially hard on low-wage workers who may have to forgo employment.

While it is not clear that support for indemnities would transfer from long-term care to Medicare, it is at least a hopeful sign that the idea of long-term care indemnities was seen as a nonpartisan effort to increase consumer choice, not as an attempt to cut benefits.

The research and evaluation team in the Cash and Counseling Demonstration was sensitive to the problem of "woodworking"— that is, verifying eligibility for the program (Simon-Rusinowitz, Mahoney, and Benjamin 1998). To be eligible, each person had to be enrolled in Medicaid, meet age and eligibility requirements, and require personal assistance services. Next, the value of the indemnity was calculated carefully for each person by one of two methods. For consumers who had been in the Medicaid waiver program for the previous six to twelve months, expenditures were averaged. For those not in the program that long, the dollar value of the waiver was calculated (Frogue 2003). Through this process of tailoring the indemnity to the client, large positive windfalls were avoided, thereby lessening the incentives for opportunistic behavior by patients and their caregivers.

Would the option of hiring previously unpaid family caregivers lead to lower quality of care and patient satisfaction? Apparently not, according to the research team (Simon-Rusinowitz et al. 2005). Among a sample of 436 clients in the "cash allowance" group in Arkansas, researchers found that approximately three-quarters were paying a family member to provide care and one-quarter were paying a nonfamily member. Not surprisingly, family caregivers were less likely to have received training in personal care, but clients with a paid family member reported receiving equal or greater assistance on all measures of assistance for which data were collected (such as help with shopping, and help with bathing or showering). Over 96 percent of consumer-directed clients in both groups reported they were satisfied with how they got along with the paid worker, but clients with a paid family member were more likely to be satisfied with the overall arrangements for care (99 percent versus 91 percent, $p < .01$).

Among the notable design features of the Cash and Counseling Demonstration, consumer-directed clients had the opportunity to use fiscal intermediaries to handle bookkeeping and payroll services on their behalf. Almost all of those in Arkansas chose this option (Simon-Rusinowitz et al. 2005). This feature also might be important in a demonstration of Medicare indemnities.

Summarizing the findings from their research, Simon-Rusinowitz et al. wrote:

> Overall, the experience of clients and their family workers in the consumer-directed CCDE in Arkansas appears to be quite positive in every area that has been of concern to policymakers. The majority of consumer-directed clients hired family workers, and those clients received equal or greater services, and experienced less unmet need, as compared to clients who hired non-family workers (2005, 103).

In 2003 the U.S. Department of Health and Human Services began the Independence Plus Initiative, another demonstration of long-term care indemnities that expands and modifies the Cash and Counseling Demonstration (Crowley 2003). One goal of this new initiative is to conduct a more thorough evaluation of consumer-directed long-term care, especially to assess the adequacy of individual budgets and the quality of care that consumers purchase with self-directed funds. The Independence Plus waivers allow states to self-direct any Medicaid service, not just services on a defined list. This program is underway in four states (Florida, Louisiana, New Hampshire, and South Carolina), and, while it is too new to have produced any conclusive findings, it indicates a continued high level of interest in long-term care indemnities.

Notes

Introduction

1. Doctors may charge up to 9.25 percent more than the allowed payments. But this just means that the total price is 1.095 times the controlled price.

2. Medicare spending is taken from Medicare Trustees, *2007 Annual Report*, 5, http://www.cms.hhs.gov/ReportsTrustFunds/downloads/tr2007.pdf. In considering how much of the Medicare budget is "price-controlled," I included payments for hospital and physician fee-schedule services but did not count any of Medicare's $6 billion in administrative expenses for Parts A and B, nor the unaccounted costs to doctors and hospitals of complying with the price controls. GDP is taken from U.S. Department of Commerce 2006.

Chapter 1: History of Medicare Physician Payment Policy

1. In insurance industry terminology, the "usual" fee stands for what is usual in the provider's practice; the "customary" fee is customary in the community; and the "reasonable" fee is reasonable for the situation (Casto and Layman 2006, 6). The adaptation of these terms to Medicare is explained by Showstack et al. (1979).

2. Robert Ball, the first administrator of Medicare, reflected on the CPR system: "We had considerable concern about such a plan but decided it was better than not covering physician services at all and that this was our only chance. So the administration supported it. We also had a naïve faith that when we had more experience with the program, we could get reasonable changes made in the law" (1998, 34).

3. See appendix 2 for a discussion of why Medicare physician payment reform took so long to come to fruition. Also see Joseph Newhouse (2001) for a discussion of the politics surrounding implementation of the Medicare

RBRVS. Although it was enacted by OBRA89, implementation of the fee schedule was put off for three years, until 1992, because of opposition from procedure-oriented specialists whose fees would be reduced. Full implementation of the RBRVS did not occur until 1996.

Chapter 2: Goal and Flaws of Medicare Physician Payment Policy

1. This claim has been made or discussed by many authors. For example, see U.S. Congress, Office of Technology Assessment (1986), Lee and Ginsburg (1988), Physician Payment Review Commission (1989), and Hsiao and Dunn (1991).

2. The "just price" is a theory of ethics in economics that attempts to set prices based on standards of fairness rather than supply and demand. Thomas Aquinas used the just price theory to argue against "usury" (charging any interest on loans). In the context of the RBRVS, what appears to be just to one patient or doctor may not appear so to others.

Chapter 3: Not-So-Real Reforms

1. The first group of Medicare patients comprises those for whom the doctor agrees to accept "assignment," meaning that he or she accepts the Medicare fee as payment in full for Part B services; the second group includes those whom the doctor balance-bills. Stephen Zuckerman and John Holahan (1991) and Robin McKnight (2007) used a similar model but did not allow physicians to charge different prices to nonassigned Medicare patients and private patients. This restriction seems odd because all of the textbook conditions for charging different prices in these two markets are met: Medicare and private patients have different and identifiable willingness to pay; physicians' services cannot be resold; and physicians have market power to set prices in both markets (Carlton and Perloff 1990, 437).

2. "Participating" physicians agree to accept assignment on all their Part B claims.

3. As discussed by Bryan Dowd et al. (2006–7), data from the 2000–2003 Consumer Assessment of Health Plans Surveys (CAHPS®) showed that about 90 percent of beneficiaries seeking new physicians reported small or no problems doing so, while special Targeted Beneficiary Surveys (TBS) commissioned by the Centers for Medicare and Medicaid Services (CMS) found that physician access generally was better for Medicare beneficiaries than for the privately insured population. These data suggest that there isn't much nonprice rationing in Medicare. Much of the case for balance billing is based on a starting point that nonprice rationing is a

severe problem. Beginning in 2004, MedPAC's *Reports to Congress* also began reporting comparisons of Medicare physician fees to those of private insurers. Although Medicare's prices were 66 percent of private fees in 1994, they were 83 percent of private fees in 2001, primarily due to a decline in private fees.

4. Prior to 1997, the maximum payment to an HMO in a county was based on 95 percent of an administrative formula known as the adjusted average per-capita cost (AAPCC), which was equal to the average Medicare reimbursement per beneficiary in the United States for that year, adjusted for historical differences in reimbursements per beneficiary in that county and the United States. The payment rate also varied with the enrollee's gender, age, reason for entitlement (age or disability), institutional status, and Medicaid eligibility.

5. Medicare Part D, enacted in 2003 and introduced in 2006, covers prescription drugs.

6. See Dowd et al. (2005–6) for a discussion of the political obstacles to past and future demonstrations of competitive pricing in Medicare.

7. As noted by Dowd et al. (2005–6), within months after passage of the Medicare Modernization Act, seven amendments had been introduced in the U.S. House of Representatives and three in the U.S. Senate to repeal the Comparative Cost Adjustment program in its entirety. In addition, twenty-five amendments had been introduced to block the demonstration in specific states or congressional districts. A political constituency for a competitive pricing system that includes FFS Medicare may not presently exist.

8. Suppose that the CCME is a nonprofit monopolist that maximizes a utility function depending on quantity and quality of care. The assumption that quality belongs in the utility function is reasonable because CCMEs will be selected, in part, based on their commitment to high-quality care. Also suppose that patients have no out-of-pocket cost-sharing, which also is reasonable for Medicare. If the CCME's budget increases, the quality of care will rise, which in turn will increase patients' demand. If the demand response to higher quality is sufficiently elastic, more generous global budgets may be accompanied by an increase in unmet demand and longer waiting lines for service.

Chapter 4: Real Reform—Medicare Indemnities

1. In a later paper, Pauly returned to the same theme. Asking, "Why does moral hazard characterize medical insurance?" he suggested again that the reason was the difficulty of defining the severity of an individual's illness once the illness had occurred (1986, 640).

2. I appreciate Ted Frech's pointing out that sickness "indemnities" were not identical to true medical indemnities that were triggered by a diagnosis on a once-and-for-all basis. Sickness indemnities provided a flow of income conditioned on continuing inability to work and, therefore, were more akin to disability insurance. Later in this chapter, however, I suggest that indemnities for chronic conditions might be paid out on a regular basis.

3. Unfortunately, Stone refers to indemnity insurance as the "disability model," while using the term "indemnity insurance" to describe the traditional policy that reimburses providers for a defined and limited set of services.

4. Pauly (2000) also discussed optimal insurance and made the same points.

5. A parallel shift in the budget line indicates that the consumer has more income, but he or she faces the same relative prices as before receiving the indemnity. In contrast, traditional insurance reduces the relative price of medical care.

6. See Zuckerman and Maxwell (2004) for an analysis of the GPCI. By law, the GPCI allows an adjustment for only 25 percent of the variation in the cost of physicians' work across local pricing areas. This limitation was based on political considerations, to equalize physician fees in low-cost rural areas with those in high-cost urban areas. There may be an economic justification, however, for not adjusting fully for local variation in the cost of physicians' work. If physicians are mobile in the long run, then the real rate of return to training should tend toward equality across local areas. Any observed differences in the cost of physicians' work would be due to "compensating differentials" (physicians need to be paid more to work in unattractive areas, for instance) or to unmeasured differences in physicians' quality and skill that vary systematically across local areas. Cutting the maximum adjustment down to 25 percent of the observed variation in costs could be seen as a way of adjusting for compensating differentials.

7. Medicare currently may approve new hospital inpatient technologies for temporary add-on payments. For a period lasting two or three years, hospitals may receive up to 50 percent of the marginal cost for patients using the new technology. Upon the sunset of the add-on payment, the prospective diagnosis-related group rates are recalibrated to reflect the use of the new technology. Since 2000, seven new technologies have been approved for add-on payments. I am grateful to Lindsay Bockstedt for bringing this point to my attention.

8. In 1991 the American Medical Association set up the RVS Update Committee (RUC) to advise the Health Care Financing Administration (now the Centers for Medicare and Medicaid Services) on new and revised codes

for the nascent RBRVS payment system. By May 1994, the RUC had made a thousand recommendations, of which 95 percent were accepted by the Health Care Financing Administration. RUC's successor, the Practice Expense Advisory Committee (PEAC), reviewed the direct practice expenses for over sixty-five hundred codes during its five-year lifespan from November 1998 to March 2004 (American Medical Association 2005).

9. Mark Pauly noted that when Blue Shield plans were first established, physicians were paid for services rendered to low-income patients according to a fee schedule that was often slightly lower than their usual charges, and they were free to bill high-income patients for additional amounts. Of interest to my discussion, he added that "the description of procedures was customarily rather broad" (Pauly 1971, 57).

10. These data represent total Medicare spending, not separated by Part A and Part B.

11. Penberthy et al. (1999) also estimated regression equations to predict cost per case and reported R^2 values ranging from .38 (prostate cancer) to .49 (breast cancer). Whether we should use the unadjusted variances from table 4-2 or the smaller variances of the residuals from the regressions to measure risk is a matter of debate. If the indemnity payments were adjusted for factors that explain cost (comorbidity, length of hospital stay, type of therapy, and ZIP-code-level income), then the variance of the regression residuals would be appropriate. However, some of the regressors used by Penberthy et al. were measures of treatment intensity, not disease severity, so they would be excluded from any adjustment to the indemnity. To be conservative, I used the unadjusted variances from table 4-2 to measure risk.

12. The conversion involves multiplying Marquis and Holmer's estimates by the Medical Care Consumer Price Index (MCPI) in 1982 and dividing by the average MCPI from 1985–88. The MCPI is taken from the U.S. Bureau of Labor Statistics at http://www.bls.gov. Marquis and Holmer's estimates apply to the population who were less than sixty-two years old at the time of their enrollment in the HIE. Some adjustment would have to be made for differences in risk aversion among the elderly and the nonelderly, but the direction of that adjustment is not clear a priori. Additional adjustment would have to be made for nonlinearity in patients' willingness to avoid risk.

13. A more complete calculation of the cost of risk-bearing would need to consider the skewness and kurtosis of costs. These statistics were not reported by Penberthy et al. (1999).

14. The amount of risk remaining after receiving the indemnity would depend on the distribution of expenses for each condition. While the details of these calculations are complicated, it is nonetheless easy to state the obvious conclusion that an indemnity equal to the average cost does not

adequately protect patients against risk. On the other hand, the extremely large total variances reported in table 4-2 imply that the distribution of risks is skewed toward a small number of very high-cost cases. By capping the patient's cost-sharing liability with a deductible for expenses above the indemnity, the risk from these rare and very costly cases could be reduced significantly.

15. The partial indemnity system recommended by Pauly resembles "tiered provider" payments used by many health insurers, in which patients pay less out of pocket if they go to a "preferred" provider who agrees to use the plan's fee schedule. The difference is that tiered indemnity payments are not dependent on choice of provider, but on the patient's total spending.

16. As of 2008, Medicare Part D beneficiaries have to pay the first $275 of drug expenses out of pocket; then they have partial coverage with 25 percent coinsurance up to $2,510 total expenses, followed by a $3,216 gap, or "donut hole," after which catastrophic coverage with 5 percent coinsurance begins. This design was roundly criticized by Meredith Rosenthal (2004), who argued that it is inefficient to put the deductible anywhere other than the lower end of the distribution of medical expenses. Putting the deductible higher up exposes the patient to more out-of-pocket risk for every dollar of premium that is saved by the deductible.

17. The following quote captures the gist of Feigenbaum's argument in favor of patient sovereignty: "When one realizes that almost 30 percent of the Medicare budget is spent on acute care during an individual's last year of life and that an alarmingly high fraction of Medicaid outlays pays for nursing home care, one suspects that the same dollars put in the hands of the ill might be spent in a substantially different way" (4).

18. She meant that they might be required to use hospice services. Strictly speaking, in an indemnity system there is no coverage for any service—the patient is paid in the event of terminal illness, but there is no list of covered services.

19. To my knowledge this externality was first analyzed by Richard Zeckhauser (1971) in the context of public programs that transfer income to the poor. Zeckhauser assumed that the donor's utility depends on the recipient's annual income and the number of hours the recipient works in a year. Therefore, holding program cost constant, the donor wishes to transfer income to the recipient in a way that does not lessen the recipient's incentive to work. For those who are able to work, the optimal plan involves a lump-sum tax and a heavily subsidized wage rate. In the Medicare context, donors would be more than happy to increase the indemnity payment (thereby holding beneficiaries' utility constant) if beneficiaries would spend more of it on medical care than on their own voluntary consumption.

20. Examples of this type of paternalism abound in the economy. Among them are restrictions on an employee's ability to receive his or her pension as a lump sum equal to the present value of expected lifetime benefits. Some employers allow this type of conversion, but require that the employee purchase a minimum annual annuity or invest the pension in one of a set of selected investments.

Chapter 6: Physician Market Power and Indemnities

1. My calculation is based on the finding by Newhouse et al. (1993, 42) that outpatient visit rates to physicians and other providers were 67 percent higher in a "free care" plan than one with a 95 percent coinsurance rate. The arc price elasticity of demand implied by this finding is $-.67$ / $[(.95 - 0)$ / $.475] = -.335$.

2. The markup is specified as $(P - MC)$ / $P = -1/n$ where n is the price elasticity of demand. So, for example, if $n = -1.75$, the markup is 1 / $1.75 = .57$.

3. Robert Town, John Kralewski, and I found that physicians tend to reject contracts with capitation payment when they have more market power, controlling for other variables (Town, Feldman, and Kralewski 2006). The implication is that declining use of capitation could be due to increasing physician market power.

Chapter 7: Let's Give It a Try

1. In 2003 Medicare paid for more than 16,353 spinal procedures, a national rate of 3.2 per 1,000 beneficiaries (Gaul 2004). Local rates of spinal surgery show wide variation, even within the same state.

2. A similar situation would arise if Medicare dropped the requirement that capitated health plans pay a tax on premium reductions. Premium rebates would be an efficient way of transferring money to enrollees, but they might not be equitable.

3. The percentage of the population spending more than $10,000 is given by $1 - F(10,000) = e^{-1} = .37$. To find how much they would have to pay out of pocket, we use another property of the exponential distribution. If you truncate it (that is, chop it off) at any value b, the mean of the remainder of the distribution is $b + E(x)$. In this case, we chop off the distribution at $10,000, and since $E(x) = $10,000$, the mean of the remainder is $20,000. This means that patients who exceed the deductible have to pay $10,000 out of pocket, on average. See Cohen (1991) for further explanation of truncated distributions.

4. The minimum deductible is zero, and the maximum is $1,000. Distributions of this type are said to be "doubly truncated."

5. The variance of out-of-pocket spending is $.37(\$1000-\$370)^2 + .63(0-\$370)^2 = \$233,100$.

Appendix 1

1. Hadley (1991) refers to physicians' marginal willingness to supply services as their "marginal cost." Baumgardner (1992) takes the view that "cost" includes the disutility of providing services.

2. Many discussions of Medicare physician pricing use "partial equilibrium" analysis, which looks at the supply and demand of one service at a time. In partial equilibrium analysis, efficiency occurs when the price of the service is at the level where supply equals demand. To determine the efficient prices for multiple Medicare services, it is necessary to use "general equilibrium" analysis. In general equilibrium analysis, consumers equate marginal rates of substitution to the relative prices of services, and providers equate marginal rates of product transformation to the relative prices. Efficient allocation of resources in a general equilibrium framework is illustrated by figure A-1.

3. Medicare does not cover all services. Until recently, outpatient prescription drugs were a good example. Most nursing home care is not covered by Medicare.

4. This point was first made by Michael Crew (1969).

5. A monopolist facing fully insured consumers will be able to set an infinitely high price. This outcome is too extreme because (a) physicians are not pure monopolists, and (b) premiums for the insurance policy will be infinitely high, driving customers away. Figure A-3 shows a high relative price of service B, but not an infinitely high price.

6. I appreciate Joe Antos's pointing out that while the "price control equilibrium" in figure A-2 and the "fully insured monopoly equilibrium" in figure A-3 both lie to the upper left of the competitive equilibrium point, they have different interpretations.

Appendix 2

1. The third layer of the 1965 legislation, passed simultaneously with Medicare, was the Medicaid program for certain low-income individuals and families who fit into an eligibility group that is recognized by federal and state law. The combination of Medicaid with the two parts of Medicare led one observer to refer to Medicare as a "three-layer cake" (DeParle 2000).

2. The Omnibus Budget Reconciliation Act of 1987 (OBRA87) had directed the Health Care Financing Administration to develop a separate relative value scale (RVS) for radiology, anesthesiology, and pathology. The American College of Radiology (ACR) played a major role in developing the radiology scale, which was implemented on April 1, 1989. The radiology RVS eventually was incorporated into the all-specialty RBRVS, but it maintained the intraspecialty relative values of the 1989 scale, rather than those developed by Hsiao and colleagues. The only other specialty to preserve its own intraspecialty relative values was anesthesiology The ACR earned bragging rights for maintaining a fee-for-service system, holding payment reductions to a level "smaller than was impending in 1987," and achieving "equitable payment within radiology—with equity determined by the organized radiology community" (Moorefield, MacEwan, and Sunshine 1993, 324–25).

References

American Medical Association. 2005. History of the RBRVS and the RUC. March 16. http://www.ama-assn.org/ama/pub/category/10559.html.

Anderson, Gerard. 2002. Untitled statement before the Subcommittee on Health, Committee on Ways and Means, U.S. House of Representatives, April 16.

Antos, Joseph R. 1991. The policy context of physician payment. In *Regulating doctors' fees: Competition, benefits, and controls under Medicare*, ed. H. E. Frech III. Washington, D.C.: AEI Press.

Arrow, Kenneth J. 1971. *Essays in the theory of risk bearing*. Chicago: Markham Publishing Company.

Atherly, Adam. 2002. The effect of Medicare supplemental insurance on Medicare expenditures. *International Journal of Health Care Finance and Economics* 2 (2): 137–62.

Ball, Robert M. 1998. Reflections on how Medicare came about. In *Medicare: Preparing for the challenges of the 21st century*, ed. Robert D. Reischauer, Stuart Butler, and Judith R. Lave. Washington, D.C.: Brookings Institution.

Baumgardner, James R. 1992. Medicare physician-payment reform and the resource-based relative value scale: A re-creation of efficient market prices? *American Economic Review* 82 (4): 1027–30.

Blendon, Robert J., Mollyann Brodie, John M. Benson, Drew E. Altman, Larry Levitt, Tina Hoff, and Larry Hugick. 1998. Understanding the managed care backlash. *Health Affairs* 17 (4): 80–94.

Berkowitz, Edward. 2005–6. Medicare and Medicaid: The past as prologue. *Health Care Financing Review* 27 (2): 11–23.

Carlton, Dennis W., and Jeffrey M. Perloff. 1990. *Modern industrial organization*. Glenview, Ill.: Scott, Foresman and Company.

Casto, Anne B., and Elizabeth Layman. 2006. *Principles of healthcare reimbursement*. Chicago: American Health Information Management Association.

Centers for Medicare and Medicaid Services. 2006. Medicare and Medicaid statistical supplement, 2004. *Health Care Financing Review*,

Baltimore, Md.: U.S. Department of Health and Human Services, Pub. No. 03469, April.

Christensen, Sandra, Stephen Long, and James Rodgers. 1987. Acute health care costs for the aged Medicare population: Overview and policy options. *Milbank Quarterly* 65 (3): 397–425.

Christensen, Sandra, and Judy Shinogle. 1997. Effects of supplementary coverage on use of services by Medicare beneficiaries. *Health Care Financing Review* 19 (1): 5–17.

Chulis, George S., Franklin J. Eppig, and John A. Poisal. 1995. Ownership and average premiums for Medicare supplementary insurance policies. *Health Care Financing Review* 17 (1): 255–75.

Cohen, Clifford A. 1991. *Truncated and censored samples: Theory and applications*. New York: Marcel Decker.

Conseco. 2008. Cancer insurance (product information). http://www.conseco.com/wsc/health/cancer.shtml (accessed March 24, 2008).

Crew, Michael. 1969. Coinsurance and the welfare economics of medical care. *American Economic Review* 59 (5): 906–8.

Crowley, Jeffrey S. 2003. An overview of the independence plus initiative to promote consumer-direction in Medicaid. Kaiser Commission on Medicaid and the Uninsured. November.

Cummins, David J., and Olivier Mahul. 2004. The demand for insurance with an upper limit on coverage. *Journal of Risk and Insurance* 71 (2): 253–64.

Cutler, David. 2002. Health care and the public sector. National Bureau of Economic Research. Working Paper 8802. February.

Davis, Karen, and Sara R. Collins. 2005–6. Medicare at forty. *Health Care Financing Review* 27 (2): 53–62.

DeParle, Nancy-Ann Min. 2000. Celebrating 35 years of Medicare and Medicaid. *Health Care Financing Review* 22 (1): 1–7.

Dionne, Georges, and Robert Gagne. 2002. Replacement cost endorsement and opportunistic fraud in automobile insurance. *Journal of Risk and Insurance* 24 (3): 213–30.

Dowd, Bryan, Robert F. Coulam, and Roger Feldman. 2000. A tale of four cities: Medicare reform and competitive pricing. *Health Affairs* 19 (5): 9–29.

Dowd, Bryan, Robert F. Coulam, Roger Feldman, and Steven D. Pizer. 2005–6. Fee-for-service Medicare in a competitive market environment. *Health Care Financing Review* 27 (2): 113–26.

Dowd, Bryan E., Roger Feldman, and Jon Christianson. 1996. *Competitive pricing for Medicare*. Washington, D.C.: AEI Press.

Dowd, Bryan, Roger Feldman, John Nyman, and Robert Town. 2006–7. Setting physicians' prices in fee-for-service Medicare. *Health Care Financing Review* 28 (2): 97–111.

Emery, George, and J. C. Herbert Emery. 1999. *A young man's benefit.* Montreal: McGill-Queen's University Press.

Etheredge, Lynn M. 1986. The volume of Medicare physician services. In *Medicare physician payment reform: Issues and answers*, ed. John F. Holahan and Lynn M. Etheredge. Washington, D.C.: Urban Institute Press.

Ettner, Susan L. 1997. Adverse selection and the purchase of Medigap insurance by the elderly. *Journal of Health Economics* 16 (5): 543–62.

Feigenbaum, Susan. 1992. "Body shop" economics: What's good for our cars may be good for our health. *CATO Regulation: The Review of Business & Government* 15 (4). http://www.cato.org/pubs/regulation/reg15n4b.html (accessed March 24, 2008).

Feldman, Roger D. 1988. Health care: The tyranny of the budget. In *Assessing the Reagan years*, ed. David Boaz. Washington, D.C.: Cato Institute.

———. 1994. The cost of rationing medical care by insurance coverage and by waiting. *Health Economics* 3: 361–72.

Feldman, Roger, Bryan E. Dowd, Robert Coulam, Len Nichols, and Anne Mutti. 2001. Premium rebates and the quiet consensus on market reform for Medicare. *Health Care Financing Review* 23 (2): 19–33.

Feldman, Roger, and Felix Lobo. 1997. Global budgets and excess demand for hospital care. *Health Economics* 6 (2): 187–96.

Feldman, Roger, and Frank Sloan. 1989. Competition among physicians, revisited: Comment. *Journal of Health Politics, Policy and Law* 14 (3): 621–25.

Feldstein, Paul J. 2001. *The politics of health legislation: An economic perspective.* 2d ed. Chicago: Health Administration Press.

Fox, Peter D. 1984. Physician reimbursement under Medicare: An overview and a proposal for area-wide physician incentives. *Proceedings of the conference on the future of Medicare.* U.S. Congress. House. Subcommittee on Health, Committee on Ways and Means. Washington, D.C.: U.S. Government Printing Office.

Frech, H. E. III. 1996. *Competition & monopoly in medical care.* Washington, D.C.: AEI Press.

———. 1999. The forgotten opportunity of reforming fee-for-service Medicare. In *Medicare in the twenty-first century: Seeking fair and efficient reform*, ed. Robert B. Helms. Washington, D.C.: AEI Press.

———. 2000. Physician fees and price controls. In *American health care: Government, market forces, and the public interest*, ed. Roger D. Feldman. Oakland, Calif.: Independent Institute.

Frogue, James. 2003. The future of Medicaid: Consumer-directed care. *Backgrounder* 1618. Washington, D.C.: Heritage Foundation. January 10.

Gaul, Gilbert M. 2004. Medicare: When geography influences treatment options. *Washington Post.* July 24.

Gianfrancesco, Frank G. 1983. A proposal for improving the efficiency of medical insurance. *Journal of Health Economics* 2 (2): 176–84.

Gillis, Kurt D., and David W. Lee. 1997. Medicare, access, and physicians' willingness to accept new Medicare patients. *Quarterly Review of Economics and Finance* 37 (7): 579–603.

Ginsburg, Paul B. 1983. Market-oriented options in Medicare and Medicaid. In *Market reforms in health care: Current issues, new directions, strategic decisions*, ed. Jack A. Meyer. Washington, D.C.: AEI Press.

Goldberg, Lawrence E., and Warren Greenberg. 1977. The effect of physician-controlled health insurance: *U.S. v. Oregon State Medical Society. Journal of Health Politics, Policy and Law* 2 (1): 48–78.

Graboyes, Robert F. 2000. Our money or your life: Indemnities vs. deductibles in health insurance. Working Paper 00-04. Federal Reserve Bank of Richmond.

Haas-Wilson, Deborah. 2003. *Managed care and monopoly power: The antitrust challenge.* Cambridge, Mass.: Harvard University Press.

Hackbarth, Glenn M. 2005a. Medicare payment to physicians. Statement before the Subcommittee on Health, Committee on Ways and Means, U.S. Congress, House of Representatives, published by the Medicare Payment Advisory Commission, Washington, D.C.

———. 2005b. Medicare payment to physicians. Statement before the Subcommittee on Health, Committee on Energy and Commerce, U.S. Congress, House of Representatives, published by the Medicare Payment Advisory Commission, Washington, D.C.

Hadley, Jack. 1984. Critique of Peter Fox's "Physician reimbursement under Medicare: An overview and a proposal for area-wide physician incentives." *Proceedings of the conference on the future of Medicare.* U.S. Congress. House. Subcommittee on Health, Committee on Ways and Means. Washington, D.C.: U.S. Government Printing Office.

———. 1991. Theoretical and empirical foundations of the resource-based relative value scale. In *Regulating doctors' fees: Competition, benefits, and controls under Medicare*, ed. H. E. Frech III. Washington, D.C.: AEI Press.

Hadley, Jack, and Robert A. Berenson. 1987. Seeking the just price: Constructing relative value scales and fee schedules. *Annals of Internal Medicine* 106 (3): 461–66.

Havighurst, Clark C. 1995. *Health care choices: Private contracts as instruments of health reform.* Washington, D.C.: AEI Press.

Hoffman, Earl Dirk, Jr., Barbara S. Klees, and Catherine A. Curtis. 2000. Overview of the Medicare and Medicaid programs. *Health Care Financing Review* 22 (1): 175–93.

Hsiao, William C., Peter Braun, Edmund R. Becker, Douwe Yntema, Diana K. Verilli, Eva Stamenovic, and Shiao-Ping Chen. 1988. *A national study of resource-based relative value scales for physician services: Final report to the Health Care Financing Administration.* Publication No. 18 C-98795/1-03. Boston, Mass.: Harvard School of Public Health. September.

Hsiao, William C., and Daniel L. Dunn. 1991. The resource-based relative value scale for pricing physicians' services. In *Regulating doctors' fees: Competition, benefits, and controls under Medicare,* ed. H. E. Frech III. Washington, D.C.: AEI Press.

Jenks, Susan. 1996. New trial empowers patients in their end-of-life care. *Journal of the National Cancer Institute* 88 (13): 865–66.

Kang, S., Y. Kwon, and C. Yoo. 2005. The effect of private insurance on health care expenditure and health utilization among cancer patients. *Korean Journal of Health Policy and Administration* 15 (4): 65–80.

Kaplow, Louis. 1994. Optimal insurance contracts when establishing the amount of losses is costly. *Geneva Papers on Risk and Insurance Theory* 19 (2): 139–52.

Knickman, James. 2005. Cash and counseling: Part of the long-term care answer? Symposium sponsored by the Kaiser Family Foundation. July 29. http://www.allhealth.org./recent/audio_07-29-05/Transcript_7-29-05.pdf (accessed April 30, 2007).

Kolata, Gina. 2006. Medicare says it will pay, but patients say "no thanks." *New York Times.* March 3.

Kotlikoff, Laurence J., and Scott Burns. 2004. *The coming generational storm: What you need to know about America's economic future.* Cambridge, Mass.: MIT Press.

Langwell, Kathryn. 1993. Price controls: On the one hand . . . and on the other. *Health Care Financing Review* 14 (3): 5–10.

Lee, Philip R., and Paul B. Ginsburg. 1988. Building a consensus of physician payment reform in Medicare: The physician payment review commission. *Western Journal of Medicine* 149 (3): 352–58.

Levy, Jesse M., Michael Borowitz, Samuel McNeill, William J. Landon, and Gregory Savord. 1992. Understanding the Medicare fee schedule and its impact on physicians under the final rule. *Medical Care* 30 (11, supplement): NS80–NS93.

Lubalin, James S., and Lauren D. Harris-Kojetin. 1999. What do consumers want and need to know in making health care choices? *Medical Care Research and Review* 56 (1, supplement): 67–102.

Mahoney, Kevin J., Kristin Simone, and Lori Simon-Rusinowitz. 2000. Early lessons from the cash and counseling demonstration and evaluation. *Generations* 24 (1): 41–46.

Marquis, M. Susan, and Martin R. Holmer. 1986. Choice under uncertainty and the demand for health insurance. Publication No. N-2516-HHS. Santa Monica, Calif.: RAND Corporation.

McGuire, Thomas G. 1991. Paralyzing Medicare's demand-side policies. In *Regulating doctors' fees: Competition, benefits, and controls under Medicare*, ed. H. E. Frech III. Washington, D.C.: AEI Press.

McKnight, Robin. 2007. Medicare balance billing restrictions: Impacts on physicians and beneficiaries. *Journal of Health Economics* 26 (2): 326–41.

Medicare Payment Advisory Commission. 2003a. *Geographic practice cost indexes.* Washington, D.C.: MedPAC. August 12.

———. 2003b. *Report to Congress: Medicare payment policy.* Washington, D.C.: MedPAC. March.

———. 2004a. *Report to Congress.* Washington, D.C.: MedPAC. March.

———. 2004b. *Report to Congress: Growth in the volume of physician services.* Washington, D.C.: MedPAC. December.

Mitchell, Janet B., and Jerry Cromwell. 1982. Physicians' behavior under the Medicare assignment option. *Journal of Health Economics* 1 (3): 245–64.

Moorefield, James M., Douglas W. MacEwan, and Jonathan H. Sunshine. 1993. The radiology relative value scale: Its development and implications. *Radiology* 187 (2): 317–26.

Newhouse, Joseph P. 2001. Medicare policy in the 1990s. National Bureau of Economic Research. Working Paper 8531. October.

Newhouse, Joseph P., and the Health Insurance Group. 1993. *Free for all? Lessons from the RAND health insurance experiment.* Cambridge, Mass.: Harvard University Press.

O'Malley, Ann S., and James C. Reschovsky. 2006. No exodus: Physicians and managed care networks. Tracking Report No. 14. Washington, D.C.: Center for Studying Health System Change. May.

Paringer, Lynn. 1980. Medicare assignment rates of physicians: Their responses to changes in reimbursement policy. *Health Care Financing Review* 1 (3): 75–90.

Pauly, Mark V. 1971. Indemnity insurance for health care efficiency. *Economic and Business Bulletin* 24 (1): 53–59.

———. 1986. Taxation, health insurance, and market failure in the medical economy. *Journal of Economic Literature* 24 (2): 629–75.

———. 2000. Optimal health insurance. *Geneva Papers on Risk and Insurance: Issues and Practice* 25 (1): 116–27.

———. 2001. Perspective: Choosing long-term care insurance. *Health Affairs* 20 (6): 109–11.

Pauly, Mark V., John M. Eisenberg, Margaret Higgins Radany, M. Haim Erder, Roger Feldman, and J. Sanford Schwartz. 1992. *Paying physicians: Options for controlling cost, volume, and intensity of services.* Ann Arbor, Mich.: Health Administration Press.

Penberthy, Lynne, Sheldon M. Retchin, M. Kathleen McDonald, Donna K. McClish, Christopher E. Desch, Gerald F. Riley, Thomas J. Smith, Bruce E. Hillner, and Craig J. Newschaffer. 1999. Predictors of Medicare costs in elderly Medicare beneficiaries with breast, colorectal, lung, or prostate cancer. *Health Care Management Science* 2 (3): 149–60.

Physician Payment Review Commission. 1987. *Annual report to Congress.* Washington, D.C.: PPRC.

———. 1988. *Annual report to Congress.* Washington, D.C.: PPRC.

———. 1989. *Annual report to Congress.* Washington, D.C.: PPRC.

Pizer, Steven D., Roger Feldman, and Austin B. Frakt. 2005. Defective design: An inconsistent approach to regional competition in the Medicare Modernization Act will be very costly to taxpayers. *Health Affairs.* Web Exclusive. W5-399–411. August 23. http://content.healthaffairs.org/cgi/search?ck=nck&andorexactfulltext=and&resourcetype=1&disp_type=&author1=Pizer&fulltext=&pubdate_year=&volume=&firstpage= (accessed March 12, 2008).

Pizer, Steven D., Austin B. Frakt, and Roger Feldman. 2003. Payment policy and inefficient benefits in the Medicare+Choice program. *International Journal of Health Care Finance and Economics* 3 (2): 79–94.

Rich, Spencer. 1988. New Medicare scale may cut some surgeon payments 30 percent. *Washington Post.* June 22.

Riley, Gerald F., and James Lubitz. 1989. Longitudinal patterns of Medicare use by cause of death. *Health Care Financing Review* 11 (2): 1–12.

Roper, William L. 1988. Untitled statement before the Subcommittee on Health, Committee on Ways and Means, U.S. Congress, House of Representatives, published by the Health Care Financing Administration, Washington, D.C.

Rosen, Harvey S. 2002. *Public finance.* 6th ed. New York: McGraw-Hill.

Rosenthal, Meredith B. 2004. Doughnut-hole economics. *Health Affairs* 23 (6): 129–35.

Ruffenach, Glenn. 1988. Big changes proposed for doctors' fees: Surgeons could get much less; G.P.s more. *Wall Street Journal*. September 9.

Russell, Louise B. 1989. *Medicare's new hospital payment system: Is it working?* Washington, D.C.: Brookings Institution.

Schwartz, Harry. 1988. Physicians' not-so-civil war. *Wall Street Journal*. February 9.

Selden, Barry J., Chulho Jung, and Roberto J. Cavazos. 1998. Market power among physicians in the U.S., 1983–1991. *Quarterly Review of Economics and Finance* 38 (4): 799–824.

Showstack, Jonathan A., B. D. Blumberg, J. Schwartz, and S. A. Schroeder. 1979. Fee for service physician payment: Analysis of current methods and their development. *Inquiry* 16 (3): 230–46.

Simon-Rusinowitz, Lori, Kevin J. Mahoney, and A. E. Benjamin. 1998. Payments to families who provide care: An option that should be available. *Generations* 22 (3): 69–75.

Simon-Rusinowitz, Lori, Kevin J. Mahoney, Dawn M. Loughlin, and Michele DeBarthe Sadler. 2005. Paying family caregivers: An effective policy option in the Arkansas Cash and Counseling Demonstration and Evaluation. *Marriage and Family Review* 37 (1/2): 83–105.

Squillace, Marie R., and James Firman. 2002. Myths and realities of consumer-directed services for older persons. National Counsel on Aging and the National Association of State Units on Aging. September.

Stone, Robyn I. 2001. Providing long-term care benefits in cash: Moving to a disability model. *Health Affairs* 20 (6): 96–108.

Strunk, Bradley, and James C. Reschovsky. 2002. Kinder and gentler: Physicians and managed care, 1997–2001. Tracking Report No. 5. Washington, D.C.: Center for Studying Health System Change. November.

Tolchin, Martin. 1989. New Medicare fees would benefit general practitioners, study says. *New York Times*. May 24.

Town, Robert, Roger Feldman, and John Kralewski. 2006. Market power and contract form: Evidence from physician group practices. Draft paper. Division of Health Policy and Management, University of Minnesota, Minneapolis.

U.S. Bureau of Labor Statistics. 1982–88. Medical care consumer price index. http://data.bls.gov/cgi-bin/surveymost.

U.S. Congress. 1986. Office of Technology Assessment. Payment for physician services: Strategies for Medicare. OTA-H-294. Washington, D.C.: U.S. Government Printing Office.

U.S. Department of Commerce. 2006. Bureau of Economic Analysis. Current dollar and "real" gross domestic product. News release, May 4.

http://www.bea.gov/bea/newsrel/gdpnewsrelease.htm.national/xls/gdplev
.xls (accessed February 28, 2008).

U.S. Department of Justice and Federal Trade Commission. 1997. *Horizontal merger guidelines*, revised April 8.

U.S. Social Security Administration. 2008. Compilation of the Social Security laws, including the Social Security Act, as amended, and related amendments through January 1, 2007. http://www.ssa.gov/OP_Home/ssact/comp-ssa.htm.

Wennberg, John E., Elliott S. Fisher, and Jonathan Skinner. 2002. Geography and the debate over Medicare reform. *Health Affairs*. Web Exclusive. February 13. W96–W114. http://content.healthaffairs.org/cgi/search?ck=nck&andorexactfulltext=and&resourcetype=1&disp_type=&author1=Wennberg&fulltext=&pubdate_year=2002&volume=&firstpage= (accessed March 12, 2008).

White, Justin, Robert E. Hurley, and Bradley C. Strunk. 2004. Getting along or going along? Health plan-provider contract showdowns subside. Issue Brief No. 74. Washington, D.C.: Center for Studying Health System Change. January.

Zeckhauser, Richard J. 1971. Optimal mechanisms for income transfer. *American Economic Review* 61 (3, part 1): 324–34.

Zuckerman, Stephen, and John Holahan. 1991. The role of balance billing in Medicare physician payment reform. In *Regulating doctors' fees: Competition, benefits, and controls under Medicare*, ed. H.E. Frech III. Washington, D.C.: AEI Press.

Zuckerman, Stephen, and Stephanie Maxwell. 2004. Reconsidering geographic adjustments to Medicare physician fees. Urban Institute. September. http://www.urban.org/UploadedPDF/411076_geo_adjustments.pdf.

About the Author

Roger Feldman is the Blue Cross Professor of Health Insurance and Professor of Economics at the University of Minnesota. Dr. Feldman was a Marshall Scholar at the London School of Economics and holds a PhD in economics from the University of Rochester. His research examines the organization, financing, and delivery of health care with a focus on health insurance. He also studies competition among health-care providers and insurers. Currently, he is evaluating the effect of "consumer-directed" health plans on medical care utilization and personal saving decisions. Dr. Feldman's experience in health policy includes serving on the senior staff of the President's Council of Economic Advisers, where he was the lead author of a chapter in the 1985 *Economic Report of the President*. From 1988 to 1992, he directed one of four national research centers sponsored by the Centers for Medicare and Medicaid Services (CMS). He advised CMS on the design of a demonstration of competitive pricing for Medicare M+C plans and, recently, provided advice to the assistant secretary for planning and evaluation (U.S. Department of Health and Human Services) on the potential for health savings accounts to reduce the uninsurance rate in the United States. Dr. Feldman is a regular contributor to journals in economics and health services research. His research has received four "best paper" awards from the Association for Health Services Research and the National Institute of Health Care Management. He has been a consultant to the U.S. Department of Justice and several state regulatory agencies regarding health plan mergers and ownership changes.

Research Staff

Gerard Alexander
Visiting Scholar

Joseph Antos
Wilson H. Taylor Scholar in Health
Care and Retirement Policy

Leon Aron
Resident Scholar

Michael Auslin
Resident Scholar

Claude Barfield
Resident Scholar

Michael Barone
Resident Fellow

Roger Bate
Resident Fellow

Walter Berns
Resident Scholar

Douglas J. Besharov
Joseph J. and Violet Jacobs
Scholar in Social Welfare Studies

Andrew G. Biggs
Resident Scholar

Edward Blum
Visiting Fellow

Dan Blumenthal
Resident Fellow

John R. Bolton
Senior Fellow

Karlyn Bowman
Senior Fellow

Arthur C. Brooks
Visiting Scholar

Richard Burkhauser
Visiting Scholar

John E. Calfee
Resident Scholar

Charles W. Calomiris
Visiting Scholar

Lynne V. Cheney
Senior Fellow

Steven J. Davis
Visiting Scholar

Mauro De Lorenzo
Resident Fellow

Thomas Donnelly
Resident Fellow

Nicholas Eberstadt
Henry Wendt Scholar in Political
Economy

Mark Falcoff
Resident Scholar Emeritus

John C. Fortier
Research Fellow

Ted Frank
Resident Fellow; Director,
AEI Legal Center for the
Public Interest

David Frum
Resident Fellow

David Gelernter
National Fellow

Reuel Marc Gerecht
Resident Fellow

Newt Gingrich
Senior Fellow

James K. Glassman
Senior Fellow

Robert A. Goldwin
Resident Scholar Emeritus

Scott Gottlieb, M.D.
Resident Fellow

Kenneth P. Green
Resident Scholar

Michael S. Greve
John G. Searle Scholar

Christopher Griffin
Research Fellow

Robert W. Hahn
Senior Fellow; Executive Director,
AEI Center for Regulatory and
Market Studies

Kevin A. Hassett
Senior Fellow; Director,
Economic Policy Studies

Steven F. Hayward
F. K. Weyerhaeuser Fellow

Robert B. Helms
Resident Scholar

Frederick M. Hess
Resident Scholar; Director,
Education Policy Studies

Ayaan Hirsi Ali
Resident Fellow

R. Glenn Hubbard
Visiting Scholar

Frederick W. Kagan
Resident Scholar

Leon R. Kass, M.D.
Hertog Fellow

Herbert G. Klein
National Fellow

Marvin H. Kosters
Resident Scholar Emeritus

Irving Kristol
Senior Fellow Emeritus

Desmond Lachman
Resident Fellow

Michael A. Ledeen
Freedom Scholar

Adam Lerrick
Visiting Scholar

Philip I. Levy
Resident Scholar

James R. Lilley
Senior Fellow

Lawrence B. Lindsey
Visiting Scholar

John H. Makin
Visiting Scholar

N. Gregory Mankiw
Visiting Scholar

Aparna Mathur
Research Fellow

Mark B. McClellan, M.D.
Visiting Senior Fellow, Health Policy
Studies and AEI Center for
Regulatory and Market Studies

Allan H. Meltzer
Visiting Scholar

Thomas P. Miller
Resident Fellow

Joshua Muravchik
Resident Scholar

Charles Murray
W. H. Brady Scholar

Roger F. Noriega
Visiting Fellow

Michael Novak
George Frederick Jewett Scholar
in Religion, Philosophy, and
Public Policy

Norman J. Ornstein
Resident Scholar

Richard Perle
Resident Fellow

Tomas J. Philipson
Visiting Scholar

Alex J. Pollock
Resident Fellow

Vincent R. Reinhart
Resident Scholar

Michael Rubin
Resident Scholar

Sally Satel, M.D.
Resident Scholar

Gary J. Schmitt
Resident Scholar; Director,
Program on Advanced
Strategic Studies

David Schoenbrod
Visiting Scholar

Nick Schulz
DeWitt Wallace Fellow;
Editor-in-Chief,
The American magazine

Joel M. Schwartz
Visiting Fellow

Kent Smetters
Visiting Scholar

Christina Hoff Sommers
Resident Scholar

Samuel Thernstrom
Director, AEI Press; Director,
W. H. Brady Program

Bill Thomas
Visiting Fellow

Richard Vedder
Visiting Scholar

Alan D. Viard
Resident Scholar

Peter J. Wallison
Arthur F. Burns Fellow in
Financial Policy Studies

Ben J. Wattenberg
Senior Fellow

David A. Weisbach
Visiting Scholar

Paul Wolfowitz
Visiting Scholar

John Yoo
Visiting Scholar